*M*ISSISSIPPI
THE BLUES
TODAY!

ROBERT
NICHOLSON

Photographs by
Logan Young

Da Capo Press
New York

A BLANDFORD BOOK

First published in the United States in 1999 by
Da Capo Press,
a Subsidary of Plenum Publishing Corporation
233 Spring Street, New York, New York, 10013

First published in the United Kingdom in 1998 by
Blandford, an imprint of Cassell plc
Wellington House, 125 Strand, London WC2R 0BB

ISBN 0–306–80883–8

Library of Congress Cataloging-in-Publication Data
Nicholson, Robert.
    Mississippi: the blues today!/Robert Nicholson; photographs by Logan Young.
      p.   cm.
    Originally published: London: Blandford, 1998.
    Includes bibliographical references and index.
    ISBN 0–306–80883–8 (alk. paper)
    1. Blues (Music) – Mississippi – History and criticism. 2. Blues musicians –
Mississippi. I. Title.
ML3521.N53 1999   98–40012
781.643'09762–dc21   CIP
                                           MN

Designed by Chris Bell

Printed in Great Britain by The Bath Press, Avon

Dedication
To Claire, who got me started.

ACKNOWLEDGEMENTS

Thank you to my commissioning editor, Stuart Booth, for his
encouragement and commitment (and for publishing the British
edition of Charles Sawyer's biography of B.B. King – the first
blues book I ever read).

A project this long in the making incurs a huge number of debts.
It would not have been possible without the help, encouragement,
hospitality and advice of James Butler, Joe Coten, Skip Henderson,
Panny Mayfield, George and Janey Newton, Carol Norman,
John Ruskey, Logan and Halle Young. Thanks to you all; and to
Eric Smith for his work on the final text.

Above all, I would like to thank the musicians themselves for
their music, their time, and their memories.

Robert Nicholson

CONTENTS

Son Thomas

Scott Dunbar

INTRODUCTION

'THE WEIRDEST MUSIC I HAD EVER HEARD'

TUTWILER, MISSISSIPPI, 1903: W.C. Handy, then a little-known cornet player from Alabama, was waiting for a train at the town's dark and deserted railroad station. His train was nine hours late and he waited, alone, until another traveller arrived and started to sing and play guitar. The mysterious black man with the old guitar sang a plaintive, moaning series of lines, repeating the same phrase three times. The guitar riff was given a strange, wavering tone by the knife he pressed down across the strings and its keening sound echoed the vocal line.

Handy's account of this strange meeting and the music he heard is the first written description of blues, the story of the music's first steps on its long musical journey. Handy called the strange sounds 'the weirdest music I had ever heard'.

Waverley Station, Edinburgh, Scotland, 1980: a skinny teenager waits for his train home from school. The station is crowded, not deserted, and the train is not nine hours late. He clutches several record albums, borrowed from school-friends or bought from any one of four favourite shops. There is the usual teenage pop (or pap?) by Blondie, the Boomtown Rats and even the Sex Pistols – and two battered, older albums that were to prove to have more immediacy, more real emotion, and a more lasting impact than the punk-pop that was supposed to have swept all that old music away.

These two old records were my own introduction to blues. They were George Thorogood's 'Move It On Over' and a compilation of the Rolling Stones' early singles – white artists' interpretations of older blues songs and tunes. It was certainly the weirdest music *I* had ever heard (my father's trad jazz records didn't count – to teenage ears they were too boring to be weird). Becoming a fan of this newly discovered music was a journey in itself, a circular journey that led back to Chicago, Memphis, and finally Mississippi, via a multitude of pubs, clubs, and bars.

◼

Those first records of mine were worn out by repeated playing and intense listening. The rhythms that the Stones and Thorogood belted out were drivingly repetitive and the musicians sounded raw and desperate. I could hear who played what and – almost – where they were in the studio during the recording sessions. Moreover, the songs promised access to a whole new world – a world where chicken was fried in bacon grease, pistols were snapped in people's faces, perfume smelt like turnip greens, and neckties were made of cobra skin. Weeping willows wept and the sky cried, and your shoes were so hot that you wished your tired feet were fireproof.

In Scotland we ate turnips (and called them 'neeps') and I had often wished for dry feet, but seldom needed them cooling down. Thus I explored this new world with a teenager's obsession and a history student's curiosity, studying the sleeve notes and writer credits, and then seeking out records by the men with the mysterious names and nicknames: E. McDaniel (and Bo Diddley too, of course, though it took longer than it should have done to link the two); Elmore James, whose incredible slicing guitar invested a musical instrument's sound with an emotion that I had never imagined possible; Chuck Berry; Willie Dixon; Muddy Waters (was that *really* his name?!).

◼

I learned that this was a music with an awareness of both its place in a community and the importance of its past – a sense of history, if you like. I also learned that many blues musicians had an acute, if usually subconscious, sense of balance: the balance between loyalty to their musical roots and the need to develop from these roots in order to prosper artistically. My exploration led directly from Thorogood and the Stones, through Chuck Berry, Muddy Waters, Bo Diddley, and B.B. King to Robert Johnson, Howlin' Wolf, and John Lee Hooker.

Recorded blues led to live blues. I listened to it in pubs, in Edinburgh and then London, at bizarre blues festivals in Hong Kong (where Japanese blues bands had no idea what they were singing about), and at yuppie coffee bars in Boston, where graduate students, clad all in black, whined country blues and plucked steel guitars. Eventually I made it to Mississippi, where I heard blues in its home environment, not disembowelled in Boston or disinfected on Beale Street, or deported in a London pub.

Mississippi – the word that had been a childhood spelling teaser – became a real place and then the apogee of my fan's journey. It was 'the land where the blues began' and it became the place where my personal musical journey was completed. When Lonnie Pitchford played his home-

made, one-string guitar, when Junior Kimborough's juke-joint lurched into its crazy, moonshine-fuelled, Saturday-night madness, when Jack Owens sang that plaintive, moaning lament, and when Booba Barnes set off on another behind-his-head guitar solo, *then* I was in the land where my blues began.

I had traced blues from Scotland to suburban London, across the Atlantic to Chicago, Memphis, and the Mississippi Delta; from a pre-eminent, world-wide position in rock music to its electrification in Chicago, and from there back to its acoustic roots as the music of the poorest, most dispossessed people of the world's richest country.

OPPOSITE:
Jack Owens'
bedroom at his
house in
Bentonia,
Mississippi.

Just as a painting or sculpture that the artist has given you personally usually has more appeal than one plucked off a gallery wall, or a bicycle that you have built yourself will be more fondly maintained than a shop-bought one, so the appreciation and understanding of music – and more especially blues – is sharpened by first-hand knowledge of the musicians and their environment. My interest was always in the artists as people, as individuals rather than as representations, force-fitted by Marxist historiography, of some economic or social trend. Hence the specifically non-academic approach to the portraits that make up this book.

Wherever possible I have tried to show how the musicians use their abilities, how these fit into their everyday lives and how they link the two, how they feel about their music and how it helps them. To all these musicians, who have opened my mind and, more importantly, my heart to the creative impulses that drive them, I owe an enormous debt of gratitude – a debt far larger than they can imagine.

I went to Mississippi as a fan, as an enthusiast who wanted to hear the music and explore the land and people who produced it. Moreover, I came as a foreigner, a non-American, and was therefore favoured with the advantages of distance and objectivity that this gave me. I approached the music, the musicians, and Mississippi itself as an outsider not weighed down or overawed by the emotional history of blues and of Mississippi. If this 'foreignness' has also manifested itself in an *apparent* disregard for the subtleties of American or more especially Southern social conventions it is due to unfamiliarity, not disrespect. But it *is* the way I saw it all.

1 Mavericks and Minstrels
A BRIEF HISTORICAL BACKGROUND

THE COUNTRYSIDE THAT nurtured the intense and heartfelt music of blues is not exhilarating or blood-stirring. It is not uplifting like the majestic beauty of the Rockies or the Scottish Highlands. It is not humbling like the enormity of the Grand Canyon or breathtaking like the Alps. It is unbeautiful – flat, plain, and unforgiving, largely a manufactured landscape. But its starkness is in keeping with the music that grew up there. What was once forested or swampy, infested with snakes, bears, and huge catfish, is now cultivated and tamed, given over to farming and human occupation. What is left undeveloped is not pleasing to the eye or soothing to the soul, just a few swampy bayous and a wood here and there. Even the big plantation houses have less ornamentation than their counterparts elsewhere in the South and few of them waste more than a small acreage of their rich agricultural land on unprofitable fripperies like lawns, shady trees, and pretty gardens.

The Mississippi Delta is not the *geographical* delta of the Mississippi river – that lies further south on the Gulf of Mexico. The Delta is the area enclosed by the Mississippi and the Yazoo rivers, roughly oval-shaped and stretching from just south of Memphis down to Vicksburg (see map).

Every spring, for each year since long before there was human habitation there, the snows to the north melted and flowed into the Mississippi, overloading the broad river's channel. Annual flooding was regular and severe, and year after year the river deposited its load of fertile silt over the flood plain – the Delta. The Delta's soil is rich and deep, perfect agricultural land that is some of the most fertile anywhere in the world. Today, however, most of the swamps have been drained and almost everywhere the land shows the taming, cultivating influence of workers of the land.

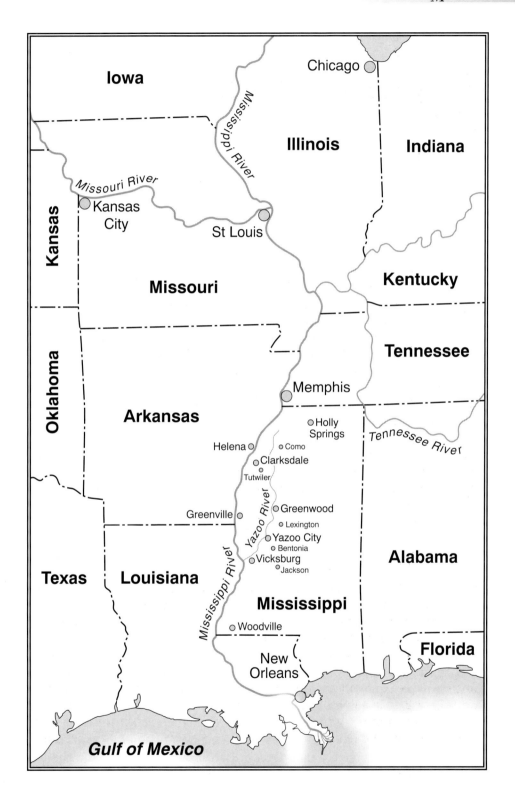

The origins of the blues are probably lost – drowned deep in a swampy, black, Delta bayou, or maybe buried under the all-enveloping kudzu weed. Most likely they are hidden for ever from the academics, folklorists, and musicologists who comb Mississippi, cheek by jowl with guided tours of Japanese blues fans. Maybe – and probably – the true origins go even further back, to West Africa, to savannah villages of pre-slavery days.

Where does a music start? What are its origins? Is it not all, in some way, a progression from what precedes it?

The documented birth of blues – its birth certificate, if you like – was at that station in Tutwiler in 1903 where W.C. Handy listened to what he later called 'the weirdest music I had ever heard'. Handy was then an unknown musician but he went on to become the self-styled 'Father of the Blues' – for that is what he entitled his 1941 autobiography, in which he tells the story of that first encounter. He became a blues Everyman: promoter, composer, writer, and all-round patron of the blues. He 'wrote' many of the most recorded and best-known of the early blues songs and was the first writer to have blues songs published. In the best blues tradition, he claimed that they were all based on songs he had heard in the fields and streets of the South as a child.

The songs were recorded by the first generation of classic blues singers, women like Bessie Smith, Ma Rainey, and Victoria Spivey. His *Blues: An Anthology* was a beautifully illustrated book of 40 of his favourite songs; published in 1931, it was to become one of the most popular and influential works of the burgeoning jazz era.

The weird sound that W.C. Handy heard on that lonely station had its roots in music that the first slaves had brought to America from Africa. This developed amidst, and was moulded by, their experience in the plantations of the Southern states and later by the harsh economic servitude of the sharecropping system that predominated in the big cotton farms of Mississippi. In the smaller farms of the hill country to the north and east of the Delta, a similar development took place.

The wailing singing and simple, repetitive rhythms are the common elements of traditional West African music and early Mississippi blues – music scholars and academics have spent hours in erudite examination of scales, polyrhythms, and chording in order to show exactly what are the common features. Early Mississippi blues was darker and starker than its East Coast or Texas counterparts; the guitar-playing was more obviously rhythmic and usually featured a knife or bottleneck being pressed on the strings to create the keening sound that Handy remembered.

Singing was heartfelt and often quite overwhelming in the depth of its emotion, and the conventional chord changes of other blues were often ignored, so that a repeated chord set up a drone, emphasizing the rhythm at the expense of the usual structure, namely, its chord progression. This can be heard in the music, from John Lee Hooker and Fred McDowell, through to R.L. Burnside and Junior Kimborough, who of today's Mississippi bluesmen most obviously display these typically Mississippian and originally African elements in blues.

With few draught animals and no wheeled wagons, everyday survival was labour-intensive in pre-colonial Africa. Coordinated effort and communal strength were needed to get a job done.

In the Mississippi Delta of the slavery and post-slavery years, labour was cheap (or free, of course) and farming was similarly labour-intensive. The field hollers that were sung to make a day's hard work easier were based on those that the original slaves had brought over from their West African homelands. Communal singing distracted from the discomfort of the Delta's choking heat and blinding light, or from the muscle-warping, bone-wrenching pain of a long day's hard, physical labour.

Yet it was also used to communicate rhythms – so that axes could be swung in time, oars pulled together, or so that two different rhythms could be coordinated. Usually, the leader of the work party would call each line or verse of the holler and the rest of the group would reply with the chorus, using the tempo of the leader's call to dictate the speed and rhythm of the work they were doing. Thus the heavy work of, say, lifting and laying railroad track could be synchronized or the different rhythms of sowing and hoeing coordinated.

This fostering of a community of cooperation was always a vital component of blues and it still is. The music was used to convey tales and messages that had a direct relevance for the listeners, who understood instinctively not only the overt content of the lyrics but also the secret subtexts that often underlay them. In Africa, drums had been used to pass messages from one village to another but in the plantations of the ante-bellum South they were banned. Blues came to take their place as message carriers. Consequently the music had a practical role to play as well as being the Saturday-night, good-time music that blotted out a week's troubles or a lifetime's sufferings.

Then, as blues developed, a new sub-class of itinerant musician grew up, separate from the rest of black society. The church-going, hymn-singing majority saw blues as the Devil's music, with the guitar as his instrument, and thus blues musicians were the lowest of the low in their society. Musicians wandered from farm to farm, from town to town, earning what they could by playing in the street during the day, and at night in juke-joints and at wild, beer- and whisky-fuelled house parties. The musicians were often homeless, like the griots in western Africa – a separate social class, respected and admired for their abilities, envied for their relative freedom, but feared and even despised for consorting with evil spirits.

In turn, the music that developed out of this harsh economic situation and searing, unforgiving countryside was, in its basic forms, very simple. Usually it was 12 bars of music, with three lines of four bars each. The singer would repeat the sung line twice and then sing a third, complementary line or he would simply repeat a line three times. This AAB or AAA rhyme scheme was accompanied by 12 bars of music with a simple chord pattern, I-IV-V (tonic, subdominant, dominant). Rhythmically it was propulsive and repetitive and, when played on guitar, the bass strings drove the rhythm underneath the melody. On faster blues, this gave dancers the obvious, insistent beat they needed to keep their feet moving. Often, each song went on just as long as the listeners still had the energy to dance, the bluesman adding verse after verse from a huge catalogue of suitable lines, a communal library of formulaic phrases borrowed, swapped, and copied from each other. Some were made up on the spot, some taken from other songs, some just slotted in because they fitted the rhythm and subject of that particular blues.

■

Charley Patton, the first of the Delta greats, was the master of these long extended blues: he could 'make a song out of anything' according to Son House. He would play the guitar between his legs or behind his head and throw it up in the air, catching it in time to continue with the next line of the blues. A consummate live performer who could keep a juke-joint jumping with 30 minutes of repeating guitar riffs, hypnotizing an audience with the rhythmic intensity of his playing, he was also the first recording star of the blues. He cut scores of tunes and most were carefully crafted and very personal tales of loving, drinking, dancing, and fighting.

Patton was a proto-guitar hero, an instrumentalist whiz-kid long before guitarists were deified. Certainly the antics and exhibitionist stagecraft of blues men like T-Bone Walker, Howlin' Wolf and, more recently, Booba Barnes have their origins in Patton's earlier example. Rock 'n' rollers like Chuck Berry and rock stars like Jimi Hendrix and scores of heavy-metal guitar players used the same flashy tricks, the same showmanship. They all owe much to this maverick minstrel of the blues.

Patton was born near Bolton, Mississippi, in 1891, or it might have been 1887 or 1885 or 1881 – the year of his birth is only one of the mysteries of his life. What is no mystery is that he grew up on Dockery's Plantation, near Clarksdale, in the heart of the Delta. By the 1920s, Charley was exasperating his God-fearing family with his guitar antics and Devil's music. He hated farm work and was soon making a living playing his music to the hundreds of black labourers on the plantation and to others in the towns and juke-joints in the surrounding area.

OPPOSITE:
A contemporary star of the blues piano tradition, Mose Vinson.

In 1929 he made the first of several recordings that were to be the influential classics on the next generation of bluesmen, just as Muddy Waters' were to be some two decades later. Son House visited Dockery's and played with the local star, as did Robert Johnson when Patton made one of his regular visits to Robinsonville where Johnson was living. Howlin' Wolf – Chester Burnett – actually came to live on Dockery's in 1926 and learned directly from Patton. His first recording was a version of *Pony Blues*, the song originally made famous by Charley, and Muddy Waters himself learned by watching Charley Patton and Son House. Thus the guitar riffs and the vocal tricks, the verses and the catalogue of blues lines were handed down from one artist to another, from one generation to the next. Lonnie Pitchford, a contemporary Delta star, learned from Robert Junior Lockwood, who, in turn, traced his inspiration back through his stepfather, Robert Johnson, and from him back to Charley Patton. Son Thomas sat in with Elmore James at a club in Yazoo County, Mississippi, learned his distinctive slide-guitar sound and was even allowed to borrow the great man's guitar. James himself had met Robert Johnson near Belzoni and based his whole career on Johnson's *Dust My Broom*.

The process continued when blues started to reach a wider, whiter audience. You can hear Howlin' Wolf trying to teach his blues to this new generation on 'The London Howlin' Wolf Sessions' when he demonstrates the slide-guitar part of *Little Red Rooster* to Eric Clapton, attempting to enlighten the man who had already built a successful career (and was reckoned to be God by many guitar players) on the back of his own imitations of Delta and Chicago blues.

Today, the learning process is often more indirect. Most of the contemporary stars of Delta blues grew up listening to the radio, where they heard not only local blues but music of all genres and from all over the country. Chicago blues, Memphis soul, big city jazz, Motown pop, West Coast psychedelia, and cajun, zydeco, gospel, and country all permeated into the Delta sound, making it harder – but never impossible – to hear the specific regional sounds of the Delta's musicians.

Lonnie Pitchford had learned Robert Johnson's *If I Had Possession Over Judgement Day* from Johnson's stepson, Robert Junior Lockwood; but he heard *My Babe* on a local jukebox and picked up Donny Hathaway's *The Ghetto*, which he covers on his 'All Around Man' album, from WJMI Radio in Jackson.

Jack Johnson listened to Hank Snow, Roy Rogers, and Gene Autry on country stations and came to love yodelling. Indeed, country music still remains a strong influence on his blues.

■

The blues riffs and songs of Mississippi were passed from one musician to the next, the successors adding their own personal touch, their own vision of the dark forces that haunted them, to the communal body of tunes, verses, and folklore.

Charley Patton's lyrics were some of the most perceptive compositions of all the Mississippi bluesmen and were closely attuned to the problems that afflicted his listeners. Robert Johnson simplified and emphasized the dance rhythms of Patton, and Johnson's boogie-woogie walking bass was to become the dominant rhythm of Chicago blues. He sang blues that were poetic in their emotional depth and feeling, and in the way they confronted the personal demons that hounded him.

Muddy Waters – McKinley Morganfield – electrified Johnson's rhythms, emphasized the sexual content of his lyrics and sparked the fire that spread the blues around the world. When he moved to Chicago in 1943, he realized that his acoustic guitar, loud enough in the juke-joints of the Delta, was fighting a losing battle in the city's noisy clubs. In 1944 he bought his first electric guitar and was soon using the extra power of the new instrument to record blues with a new physical presence. With the electric instrument's extra volume came a greater scope to emphasize the tones of Delta blues – the lights and shades, the nuances that made the music so moving. He put together a series of crack bands and took Delta blues to its next progression – by harnessing the amplified power of the bands' musicians to create a huge, tight, hard-driving sound with a pronounced physical impact. It was perfect for the fast life of the city. Delta blues had always been good-time, forget-about-your-troubles, Saturday-night music, and now, up in the big city, it was expanding to fulfil the same function as it had in the jukes and on the plantations of the Delta.

Between 1940 and 1950, Chicago's black population increased by 70 per cent and these newcomers lapped up the new blues sounds. The mill hands and steelworkers of the city rocked just as hard to the citified, electric blues of Muddy Waters as the sharecroppers of Mississippi had to the Delta blues of Robert Johnson. Blues still flourishes in the bars and clubs of Chicago. Many blues musicians capitalize on this by opening blues clubs of their own – Buddy Guy has a club called Legends.

Muddy was the king of Chicago blues for over a quarter of a century, the star who inspired the white rock 'n' rollers and who took the music from its local minority audience into the pop charts of the world. His hit songs on the Chess label were covered by the likes of the Rolling Stones (Muddy later returned the favour with an extraordinary version of their *Let's Spend the Night Together*), the Yardbirds, John Mayall's Bluesbreakers, the Paul Butterfield Blues Band – and later by almost every pub and bar band who claimed, however spuriously, to play the blues. *Got My Mojo Working* must be the most covered song in the whole Muddy Waters canon and other cover-band favourites are *Hoochie Coochie Man*, *Mannish Boy*, *Rollin' and Tumblin'*, and – of course – *Rolling Stone* itself.

Detroit was not far behind Chicago as the favourite destination for the northward-migrating Southern blacks. Chicago had steel foundries, heavy industry, and huge meat-processing plants, but Detroit had its own industrial giant in the motor-vehicle industry, which was especially resurgent during World War II when it was turning out thousands of tanks for the war effort. While the blues alley of Chicago's South Side was Maxwell Street, in Detroit it was Hastings Street, home to most of the city's best blues clubs and musicians. John Lee Hooker headed straight there when he arrived from the South; his *Boogie Chillun* recounts that arrival:

> When I was first into town, people, I was walking down Hastings
> Street. Everybody was talking about Henry's Swing Club, I decided
> I'd drop in there tonight . . .

John Lee Hooker was born in the Delta near Clarksdale in 1917, but arrived in Detroit in 1943, having spent much of the intervening time in Memphis and Cincinnati. He wasted no time in finding evening work, playing guitar in the bars of Hastings Street, while working days as a janitor in a factory. John Lee was always ambitious and he made sure that his unique, primitive sound – allied to a nice line in sly, knowing, and thoroughly modern lyrics – soon attracted the attention of record-label owners. In 1948 he cut *Boogie Chillun* for local promoter Bernie Bessman. It was distributed nationally through Modern Records and became a big hit, selling over a million copies. Another million-seller, *I'm in the Mood*, followed in 1951 and Hooker has recorded prolifically ever since. *Dimples* was a big hit in 1964 and his collaborations with West Coast rock band Canned Heat in the early 1970s were commercial and artistic successes.

Latterly, of course, he has become a bestselling recording star all over again, assuming the role of 'wicked old uncle of the blues' to that of B.B. King's as 'King of the Blues'. He has enjoyed a series of hit albums and high-profile partnerships with younger stars of the blues and rock world: Robert Cray, Bonnie Raitt, Carlos Santana, Van Morrison, Canned Heat (again), George Thorogood, Los Lobos, Ry Cooder, Johnnie Winter, Albert Collins, and Keith Richards have all appeared on his albums since 1989.

His 1991 album 'Mr Lucky' did well on both sides of the Atlantic and reached No. 3 in the UK album charts, the highest position ever by a blues record (and, at 74, John Lee was the oldest man ever to get that high a chart slot). He has also starred in several internationally broadcast TV commercials. He deserves to be enjoying this Indian summer of artistically and financially fulfilling old age. He lives in San Francisco, comforted by the city's laid-back cosmopolitanism, and still has the energy to appreciate its pretty waitresses. You can certainly hear the gleeful joy with which he introduces the last two minutes of *Boogie on Russian Hill* on his 'Boom, Boom' album.

OPPOSITE:
Cedell Davis,
a modern
inheritor of the
Delta blues
sound.

'Look, people, this is a long-playing album, you can party all night!' he sings, freed to cut loose on an extended track as he had never been on the badly rewarded, hastily recorded three-minute singles of his early career.

The Hooker sound is straight out of Mississippi. The guitar boogie and unmistakable vocal growl are always there whoever the back-up musicians may be. He plays repetitive, minimal guitar and often repeats one chord for as long as he feels like it, extending a blues for as long as it takes to finish telling a story. Sometimes he repeats a single word again and again, wrenching from it every shade of meaning and every last nuance of emotion. Just listen to him on B.B. King's 'Blues Summit' album to hear him singing some of the deepest Delta blues, repeating 'you, you, you, you' to great effect on *You Shook Me*.

His eccentric timing has always made it hard for a band to follow him – on his early records for Bernie Bessman he was usually recorded solo. He played guitar and stamped out the time with his foot and, eventually, Bessman gave him a wooden platform with a microphone rigged up beneath it to amplify his eerie, echoing stomp. His one-chord-drone blues still creates an almost hypnotic trance and is openly emotional in a way that could never be confused with the lighter style of, say, Lightnin' Hopkins.

Strangely, for one who has so often been such an unreformed old-style purist, Hooker has been covered and accompanied by an eclectic mix of superstar rock acts. Canned Heat, Van Morrison, and the Animals all found their original inspirations in blues and are less surprising Hooker fans than Bruce Springsteen, for example, who recorded *Boom Boom* for his live double album. Perhaps it is simply that the Delta elements which Hooker has retained and emphasized are the same as those popularized by the rock music of the 1950s and 60s – the simple repetitive rhythm, the danceability of the sound, and the relevant, accessible lyrics.

While the contemporary strains of Delta and Mississippi blues developed in Chicago, Detroit, and St Louis and from there conquered the world, the musicians who remained in the Delta – and there were some, despite the great exodus northwards – continued to live their lives and make their music. The blues revival of the 1960s refocused attention on the Delta.

The researchers and folklorists who put up with the climate, the segregation and the indifference, or outright opposition of local whites to seek out 'undiscovered' blues players were, by and large, less interested in contemporary Delta blues. What they wanted were survivors of an older, supposedly dying, tradition. 'Discoveries' like Skip James, Fred McDowell, Son House, Mississippi John Hurt, and Bukka White were all fêted – acclaimed as the last exponents of a pure 'folk blues' sound. They gained varying degrees of financial reward and artistic revitalization through white audiences at colleges, festivals, and concert halls, who took to them with rapt attention and blind devotion. Yet this concentration on old-style, 'pure' folk artists also served to detract attention from what was still a vibrant, contemporary scene.

The contemporary scene is still alive today. Although there are the more traditional artists of the type that the folklorists flocked to see in the 1950s and 60s, there are also thoroughly modern artists who will develop their art and the music they play to its next stage – just as Charley Patton, Robert Johnson, Muddy Waters, and B.B. King did before them.

In Mississippi, kids listen to rap music, but in the clubs and juke-joints of Clarksdale, Shelby, Greenville, and Holly Springs, it is blues that still provides the musical means for adults – young and old alike – to forget their troubles and enjoy their weekends. Juke-joints are rocking and rolling on Friday and Saturday nights, when these local artists play for what are largely local audiences.

Most of the 'rediscovered' artists may have passed away but, still, 'the blues is all right'. New generations of Delta bluesmen continue the Mississippi music tradition that is still enjoyed by the local audiences whose fathers and mothers, grandfathers and grandmothers enjoyed it in previous generations. The huge plantations are now largely mechanized and many have been sold to multinational investment corporations. The sharecropping lifestyle that was the social backcloth to the development of the music is gone but blues is blues and jobs are still hard to come by, times are still tough, and there is still a price to pay for love.

The civil rights movement may have swept away the legal foundations that maintained the institutionalized racism of the South, but in many places attitudes have not changed and much of the black population of the Delta is still consigned to its place on the other side of the tracks, condemned to the life of a second-class citizen in the land where 'all men are created equal'.

So, of course, men and women will always get the blues when hearts get broken and when there's 'midnight prowling going on'. As John Lee Hooker says, 'When Adam and Eve first saw each other, that's when the blues started,' and for as long as we all create our own little versions of Eden's apple, then the blues will still be sung.

2 DIDDLEY-BOW TO DINNER SUIT

LONNIE PITCHFORD

My baby, she don't stand no cheating, My babe,
My baby, she don't stand no cheating, My babe,
She don't stand none of that midnight creeping . . .

THE WORDS OF THE old Willie Dixon classic are familiar from dozens of live and recorded versions but tonight, as they float gently into the balmy Delta night, they sound different. It's as though they have just been composed and 'my babe' is a favourite girlfriend, a real person, not just a character in a song. The song is renewed with a substantial, personal meaning. Yet the singer is not Eric Clapton with all-star backing musicians at London's Royal Albert Hall, nor even a Chicago star with a top band at a club on the South Side. It's Lonnie Pitchford, a young and little-recorded blues artist singing in his living-room and playing not a guitar but a diddley-bow, the home-made, one-string instrument on which so many old-time blues players first learned.

Lonnie lives in Lexington, Mississippi, a small town in the southern part of the Delta. While, as a European writer and visitor, one feels able to say that it is similar to scores of others all over the 'Deep South', equally one must also observe that beyond the glitz of Atlanta's Olympic developments and the regeneration of Memphis, there is another South, another United States where the wealth of the world's richest country has had very little impact. All over the Delta, in small towns like Lexington, the untruths of the modern American dream are laid bare – the myth that we know from Hollywood movies, prime-time TV and tourist brochures is exposed.

Significant parts of the country resemble the Third World in terms of their poverty: throughout the state of Mississippi there are communities that lack the basic amenities which most of the rest of the USA has taken for granted for over 40 years. It is still the poorest state in the nation. Yet Lonnie and his wife, Minnie, are lucky – they have running water and electricity; many of their neighbours do not.

I'd called Lonnie from Memphis earlier in the day to remind him that we were coming down. We had needed travel directions.

'Man, you'll never find it on your own. Meet me at the Double Quick gas station and I'll show you the way,' he had said.

We sorted out some arrangements for the interview. Lonnie said, 'I'm real poor, man . . . you know how I spell interview? "M-o-n-e-y"!'

However, we suggested that you could also spell it 'B-e-e-r' and Lonnie liked the sound of that too.

It was dusk when we got to Lexington and our big VW camper van was conspicuous – it stood out like the owner's new car in a decrepit, second-hand car lot. Lonnie doesn't drive, so we followed him in his friend's car down dark, badly surfaced roads, past rickety, wooden houses whose peeling paint and overgrown bushes created a palpable aura of neglect. Kids in baggy shorts and baseball caps were still playing basketball in front of the houses and mangy dogs were scrapping amongst the chicken bones.

Lonnie and Minnie's house seemed to me a strange mixture of old and new; old home-made and brand-new shop-bought. They had a new sofa which was still wrapped in its plastic protective sheeting, too clean and new for everything around it. They were using an upturned beer crate as a makeshift table.

'So, are we gonna do the interview? Man, you know I HATE interviews.'

'So do we, Lonnie. Let's just drink some of this beer and relax here.'

Lonnie Pitchford is in his early forties, but he has a mischievous grin and pointed ears that make him look much younger. He's an established star of the specialist blues scene in the Southern states of the USA, and plays at festivals and clubs up and down the country. He's also played abroad several times, mainly in Europe but also in Australia. Recently he has recruited a band to play a more contemporary style of Delta blues but he really made his name playing traditional Delta blues on acoustic guitar or on the diddley-bow.

Lonnie's father, Willie Douglas Pitchford, or 'W.D.' as he was known, was also a guitarist but would not let Lonnie play his guitar so, like so many others before him, Lonnie improvised. When he was five, he rigged up a home-made one-string guitar – a diddley-bow – and taught himself to play, copying the music he heard around him. He seems to have had a natural talent for music because he learned very quickly and was soon playing in a school band. When he left, he set up his own band, which played at local clubs and bars. Lonnie would brave the Saturday-night juke-joint fights and wake up the next day to play guitar behind a church vocal group. He was already an accomplished guitarist when he met Robert Junior Lockwood.

'Robert Junior, man, he taught me tunings,' Lonnie remembers.

These open tunings enabled him to transfer his skills with a slide and a diddley-bow onto a six-stringed instrument. The survival and growth of blues has traditionally been nurtured by one generation of players handing their musical skills and techniques on to the next. Lonnie claims Eugene Powell as his main teacher: 'I'm still learning off him. He's a walking "encyclo" of the blues.'

Many of his festival performances start with a demonstration of how to make a diddley-bow. He makes one on stage and then uses the new instrument to play a selection of blues that includes heartfelt, personal versions of Robert Johnson's most haunting songs. His talent is such that he is now in demand all over the world. When we met him, he had recently returned from a tour in Australia.

'I wrestled a twenty-foot crocodile, I did.'

'Man, come on . . . I can hardly believe what he's saying. My scepticism obviously shows.

'You think I'm lying?'

'No! No, what I think is next time you go to Australia, call me up 'cos I wanna go with you!'

'They tape his mouth and then you gotta hang on. He can't bite you 'cos his mouth is taped.'

'But if you let go his tail would still get you . . .'

'Yeah, but his tail can't kill you.'

'No, but it can hurt you. How big was it?'

''Bout twenty feet long. Looked like it had a mouth that it could swallow a boat with.'

■

Lonnie claims that Minnie is Elmore James' daughter.

She says she is not so sure: 'My mom used to go with Elmore,' she says, but claims no more than that.

Traces of a host of blues legends certainly run through Lonnie's playing. There is the haunted, self-absorbed fear of Robert Johnson, the manic slide-guitar energy of Elmore and the more recent, more direct influence of Robert Junior Lockwood. But there is no need for Lonnie to use Minnie's relationship to Elmore James to boost his own position in the blues pantheon: his intense lifestyle, impassioned live performances, and acclaimed first album reveal a blues talent that is sufficient for Lonnie to lay claim to this status in his own right. The spirited musical reaction to repression and poverty that has grounded blues for decades still drives him; this Delta lifeforce that links him and his family to their past and to their ancestors still succours them in their present struggle.

■

OPPOSITE:
Lonnie
Pitchford with
one of his
home-made
instruments.

I slapped the roach off the inside of my thigh before it crawled up my shorts. Roaches were scampering all over the floor and up the walls but we were just beginning not to notice. We'd had a few beers, and we were just

getting a hold on Lonnie's weird brand of word-play and jive talk. Every time he went out of the room he would reassure us with: 'It's all white, I'll be right black!' He also said 'Gobbledegook' at odd, seemingly random, moments of conversation. His imitation of accents is exactly right; he did my English accent perfectly, calling me 'Robot' because, he says, that's how *I* said it when I introduced myself.

We were desperate to hear him play.

'Man, I've got no guitar' he repeated. He told us that, because this was a rough area and he didn't want his valuable guitar to be stolen, he had given it to an ex-sheriff who was keeping it safely inside his house. 'You don't go round visiting a man like that in the middle of the night,' Lonnie said, 'else he's liable to shoot you!'

Well, that was that. Or it would have been with any other guitarless guitarist. But not with Lonnie. He went out on the back porch to find a broom so that he could demonstrate his speciality. He was going to make a diddley-bow.

'I found a broom and, you know, Minnie, you need a new broom anyway!'

'Lonnie, that ain't my broom.'

'Then it's a stolen broom. We got a hot broom!'

Extracting the nail that held the wire onto the broom's handle was not easy. Lonnie nearly cut his finger off with a dangerous-looking Japanese kitchen knife. On TV, they claim it can cut through steel – it certainly looked like it could manage mere skin and bone. But Lonnie prised the nail out and unwound the wire. 'Well, they'll never recognize their broom now!' He hammered a nail into the top of the door frame and another into the bottom. He stretched the wire tight between them, put a shower head underneath it, and tested it with his finger to tune it. He found a glass bottleneck and a matchstick and started to play the new instrument:

'My baby, she don't stand no cheating, My babe,
My baby, she don't stand no cheating, My babe,
She don't stand none of that midnight creeping. . .'

Lonnie's voice is light: expressive through delicate qualities of shade and tone, rather than through power and force, it skips, feather-light, across the top of the melody. We were all stunned that such seemingly casual playing and singing could sound so purposeful, so alive and full of emotion.

'Ain't no one make that talk like Lonnie. He's creative. He's a genius!' says his brother-in-law.

'Wow!' is all I can manage.

'Woooeee!'

Even Minnie is stunned: 'That [diddley-bow] will never move as long as I live!'

Lonnie and Minnie have known each other for 20 years: 'Oh my.

I started going with him when he was kid, between 17 and 19 years. He didn't even know what women was about! I came down from Chicago visiting my mom's house and Lonnie was there playing guitar with my mom's old man. I took a liking to the kid.'

She already had kids of her own so, when they got together, he inherited a large extended family. Several of them come in and out as we speak – daughters, in-laws, cousins, uncles, and aunts. Minnie grew up with the blues and is well aware of Lonnie's potential. She's still desperate for him to develop it: 'I'm behind his music 100 per cent. I think I'm the biggest fan he got.'

Lonnie sets quite a pace on the partying front. We drank our share of beer, but struggled to keep up with him and I thought of Little Walter, Robert Johnson, and Magic Sam – other bluesmen who have lived fast and died young. So many seem to need to live dangerously in order to fuel the creativity that makes such impassioned music – like having to stand too close to the edge of a cliff in order to appreciate the beauty of the view. Lonnie has already had arguments with his management, who disapprove of his lifestyle. He makes the point very strongly that no one tells them how to live *their* lives. They have their vices just as he has his: 'I do what I want to do, you do what you want to do.' Right, I'm thinking, but do we really need to traipse across Lexington in the middle of the night to barter with a shady-looking man in a mobile home just because we have run out of booze and Lonnie wants to party till dawn? Lonnie had to catch a bus to a gig in Atlanta the next day and that early-morning trip to the Greyhound station loomed ever closer. Let's hope he'll catch that bus in the morning and get to his gig on time. When we retired to the camper van, we left Lonnie and his newly enhanced energy. He was still pepped up and ready to argue vociferously with Minnie till the sun came up.

I probably shouldn't have worried about that bus. At about nine the next morning Lonnie and Minnie woke us with offers of black coffee and malt liquor. 'Come on, Oprah's on the TV. Time to get up.' Instant coffee, Colt .45, and Oprah Winfrey. Now that was a breakfast combination I'd never been offered before. I accepted just the coffee.

We took Lonnie and Minnie to the Greyhound stop. We were late, of course, and needed to stop off on the way so that Lonnie could pick up his guitar. He asked us to stop in the main square of Lexington, outside a pawnshop. So that's where the guitar was. Perhaps the ex-sheriff was also a pawnbroker! Guitar successfully unhocked, Lonnie wanted to pose for some pictures at the bus stop. He did not look very photogenic – his 'Original Kick Butt' sweatshirt and jeans were dirty, his 'morning after' eyes were squinted against the sun and his beard needed a trim – but he still did not look as bad as I felt. Perhaps Oprah cures hang-overs after all.

The next time I saw Lonnie he was wearing a black tuxedo and his beard was neatly outlined, freshly shaved. He was in Memphis, not Lexington, and he was playing the piano at Justine's, the smartest restaurant in the city. It is a very swanky place, a luxury French restaurant in a large old mansion house. The hostess greets the customers in a long evening gown and the waiters make valiant efforts to pronounce the name of each dish in their best French. The entrance hall is sumptuously decorated with velvet curtains over every window and a polished grand piano in pride of place by the dining-room entrance. Inside the dining room the tables are covered in immaculately pressed white tablecloths and the menus on them are all handwritten in French.

An enlightened patron of Justine's had sensed the congruity of the best restaurant and the best blues and organized for Lonnie to play the guitar at Justine's for a friend's birthday party. Lonnie had arrived on time and looked splendid in his hired tuxedo. Unfortunately his equipment was no match for his appearance and his amplifier had blown. Someone was despatched to find a music store that was open late and could lend another, and in the meantime the customers in the dining room went back to their escalopes and their foie gras. Those in the hall who were waiting to be seated drank their aperitifs and told each other about their BMWs. Lonnie had been hired to play and was not going to waste an opportunity like this so he sat straight down at the huge grand piano. He began to play an exquisitely delicate piece of music that silenced the chitchat in the hall and stunned the rest of us who knew only that he could play any kind of guitar and could sing like an angel but sometimes behaved like a devil. I don't think anybody had heard him playing a piano.

It was a simple tune but Lonnie played it with a jazz man's feel for improvisation and a bluesman's awareness of musical structure. The pull between these two created a tension in the melody and the rhythm that was captivating. He played slowly, delaying the chords to emphasize them, as an electric guitarist sustains the notes of a solo. The emotion in Lonnie's playing was communicated by this delay, by this brave but entirely appropriate timing. Lonnie sounded more at home in the swish surroundings of Justine's than any of the braying, gold-card-carrying urban professionals who seemed to make up the majority of the restaurant's customers – his piano-playing was the only thing there that approached the artistic heights of the Impressionist paintings on the walls or the French brandies that the waiters were dispensing in the dining room.

Lonnie has done a version of the song, which he calls *My Sunny*, on 'All Around Man', his recent album. In the sleeve notes he says it is a song to relax to, to lie back with your girlfriend and drink cognac to! On record it is almost as stunning as it was live: soaked through with a (short but full) lifetime's experience, it is at once soothing and thought-provoking, like a walk in the rain when times are hard and 'the blues creep upon you and carry your mind away'.

My Sunny is one of the 19 tracks on the album, which offers an enticing summary of Lonnie's talents and his versatility. He plays acoustic and electric guitar (slide and rhythm), bass, diddley-bow, piano, and claves on it. He sings, of course, and even does a convincing vocal imitation of a harmonica! The more familiar acoustic material that he is best known for has a strongly African feel on the album: on the version of *My Babe* the diddley-bow sounds almost like an mbira, the finger piano of African traditional music; on *55 Blues* Lonnie's acoustic slide-playing shakes and vibrates like a banjo or even a halam, the West African five-stringed instrument that is played with an open, vibrating drone string.

It is the more unusually arranged songs, though, that show the true breadth (and depth) of his talent. On the band version of *If I Had Possession Over Judgement Day* the drums and bass pull the song along with a sinewy grace which is closer to funky jazz fusion than the straight blues of the original (or of the solo version that is also on the album). On Donny Hathaway's *The Ghetto* Lonnie shows off his jazz chops and lays down some smoky, late-night bar guitar soloing on top of the rhythm section's groove. It's certainly a development from the 'Robert Johnson acolyte' style for which Lonnie has become known.

The way I see it, Lonnie Pitchford's blues is not revivalist music preserved, like a dead fish in formaldehyde, at Northern colleges and clubs, and at outdoor festivals. It is not a socio-economic phenomenon to be studied by sociology professors and dry academics, preserved as a museum piece with a label 'Folk Music – indigenous to Mississippi Delta, 1910–50: the musical protest of poor black sharecroppers against their socio-economic conditions.' It is a living, developing music, a means of expression for Lonnie and his neighbours, who are still some of the most dispossessed and least powerful groups of society (just as rap music is for another, much larger group in the USA). They have few other means of protest or expression. It is also Lonnie's job, his craft and his art; and although it was nurtured and supported by festival organizers and academics, it has grown beyond them. It stands on its own, his unique artistic expression of surviving.

3 *T*HIS AIN'T NO BEALE STREET

BOOBA BARNES

*T*HANKFULLY THE SHOUT came from the other side of the street, but the words were directed at us with sullen animosity and unmistakeable menace. 'This ain't no fucking Beale Street, man. What'ya doing here? This ain't the place for you, man.'

We stood taller and walked quicker. We'd heard theme park blues in the tourist trap that is Beale Street and had come here to Greenville, Mississippi, to hear the real thing in its native environment. The violence implicit in the shouted threat suggested that we might have been better staying on Beale. The violent crime, the crack dens, the thieves, and the junkies – all of my imagined horrors of American city ghettos – were here in close-up and it was not the close-up of a TV documentary or a newspaper feature, but the stark, scary close-up of reality.

I thought of the warning we'd been given earlier that day: 'It's wild down in Nelson Street. I wouldn't go down there.' We were at the Delta Blues Festival just outside Greenville and were trying to line up our evening entertainment. 'Booba Barnes is playing there tonight and I really wanna see him but Nelson Street's pretty bad now. I don't really wanna go down there.' I remember taking the warning personally, but not very seriously. Who did this guy think he was, spoiling our anticipation of a good night out with his tame lack of adventure? He wore pressed jeans, clean hiking shoes and had camera bags weighing him down on both shoulders. I summed him up, quickly and uncharitably, as an academic type, probably another professor of social ethnomusicology who was 'studying' the blues. We wouldn't be heeding any of his warnings.

'Another guy got shot there last night, I heard,' he added.

'Shot?' That sounded serious.

'Yeah, seems like he was at a red light, and they just opened the door and pulled him out of his car.' My own sense of adventure began to seem foolhardy.

He pointed his fingers at me like a pistol, 'BANG! They just shot him! And they'll be ready for lots of tourists from the festival tonight.' His words carried less conviction three hours later when we'd had a few more beers and been seduced by Koko Taylor's brand of blues raunchiness. We ignored the warning, of course, because that's what warnings are for when you've been in the sun all day, listening to blues and drinking beer.

Nelson Street is the main entertainment drag of Greenville, which is the largest river port in the Mississippi Delta. The street has long been famous for blues music, vice dens, and for all the other wild things that go on in ports all over the world. The street is lined with clubs and bars and is still a thriving centre of entertainment on a Saturday night. Unfortunately, crack has sent crime rates soaring in this city, as it has in so many others, and most of it is crime with a frighteningly casual, but very intense, level of violence.

Roosevelt 'Booba' Barnes was a local musician who had made his name in Greenville, before leaving for the blues big-time in Chicago. He was born just south of the city, near Longwood, in 1936. He learned the harmonica when he was only eight and was soon playing locally in a gutsy, Howlin' Wolf style. By the late 1950s he led his own band and then set about learning the guitar because he could not find a guitarist who backed up his harmonica-playing with just the sound he wanted. Guitar became his premier instrument although he still played the harp on occasions.

We had just parked the VW van in the least dark parking lot we could find and paid a guy five bucks to watch it. We set off down the busy street with no real idea of which club Booba Barnes was playing in or even if he was playing at all. Huge old Cadillacs, Chevys, and pick-up trucks charged up and down and groups of young men and women dashed about, waving at each other, and shouting at us, 'This ain't no fucking Beale Street, man. What'ya doing here? This ain't the place for you, man.'

I pulled out my flask and we all had a sip of whisky. The liquor calmed our nerves only a little. We headed for the biggest club with the loudest music.

'Where's Booba playing tonight, then? Is he playing here?'

A giant disguised as a bouncer stood in the door, making no move to let us pass. His square-shouldered bulk blocked the view into the club. 'Not here. He ain't playing here.'

We wandered further down the street, ignoring more shouts. At least the whisky was having an anaesthetizing effect – it certainly took the edge off the tension and numbed our fear a little. At the bottom of Nelson was a tiny club called Lily's Lounge. An unlikely looking place, it was tucked away at the quieter end of the street. It had a porch and a front garden that made it look like a house; only the neon sign above the door indicated

otherwise. Surely Booba wouldn't be playing in a dive like this? But he was, so we paid the man on the door and went inside, where we were met by Lily herself, resplendent in a shiny cocktail dress and with a bouffant hair-do in a strange, unnatural shade of smoky pink.

'Come on in, boys. Let me get you a table. D'you want some beers?' She got us four quart bottles of Budweiser and confirmed that this was where Booba was playing. Lily's welcome could not have contrasted more with the one which we'd received out on Nelson Street itself.

We settled at our rickety, Formica-covered table with its legs of at least two different lengths and drank our beers. Their coolness was refreshing and it sharpened the lazy warmth of the whisky. The club was as small as it had looked: it was roughly rectangular, and it had no stage, just a cleared area for the band at one end, 15 or 20 small tables in the middle, and a pool table at the back. The floor was covered in linoleum so worn that it could never look clean, however much Lily and her help scrubbed it. Most of the tables were loaded down with quart beer bottles like the ones we were drinking from.

The club was not what you would call full: I counted 37 people excluding us. Within 15 minutes we seemed to have been personally welcomed by most of them: 'Hi. Hello there. How're you doing? Whatcha doing here? Where you from?'

■

Lily went to the microphone to introduce Booba and the band, but not before she had made us feel comfortable: 'We've got some guests from out of town here tonight. Where you from, boys?'

'Memphis,' the others answered.

'Scotland,' I shouted, which got blank looks from Lily, so I tried again: 'England.'

'Wow! Well, you are from outta town! I'd like y'all to make our guests here very welcome. They come a long way to be here tonight. Now here's Booba and the boys.'

On they came. Booba had a lean, healthy look about him: he was nearly sixty but looked much younger. As he swaggered up to the microphone, the lights on the low ceiling caught the shine in his extravagant purple suit and sparkled on his gold jewellery. No doubt he had picked up some style tips from the sharp-suited city slickers up on the South Side in Chicago. He milked the attention, making the most of being the homecoming son, the local lad made good.

His band, the Playboys, were a bass player, a drummer, and a rhythm guitarist, who was the only other white guy in the club. In his old jeans, boots, and a plaid work shirt he looked like he should have been playing for a Southern boogie band – the Allman Brothers Band or Lynyrd Skynyrd. The Playboys were a solid, no-frills band and a good complement to

OPPOSITE:
Booba Barnes at the Gloucester Blues Festival – one of his last performances.
Tim Spencer

Booba's more expansive style. He had a charismatic stage presence with wild eyes and a 'don't mess with me' stare that he fixed on the audience like Chuck Berry used to do. I was not surprised to hear later that the Playboys had broken up with much recrimination and ill-feeling soon after this Greenville gig. The dispute had come to a head when Booba delved into a pocket of one of his flashy suits and pulled a pistol on the drummer.

This gig at Lily's Lounge was special for Booba because he had recently sold what he had and moved to Chicago. Greenville was his home town and he used to own a joint further up Nelson Street called The Playboy Club. He says he moved north because 'it puts me a little closer to the places I go and play at'. He's much in demand: in Boston, New York, and the East Coast as well as Chicago. Here he was welcomed as a favourite son who had left town and made his fortune in the big city.

■

Booba Barnes played the guitar with a harshness and a mean menace that mirrored the real-life violence of the world outside. It is a modern style: he played single-string lead runs that were strongly reminiscent of the original West Side guitarists like Otis Rush, Buddy Guy, and Magic Sam. He did not play the guitar until 1958; his first instrument was the harmonica and by the age of 13 or 14 he had developed a Howlin' Wolf-influenced style that was accurate and competent enough to gain recognition from the man himself. Booba had the confidence of youth and persuaded Wolf to let him sit in one night at a juke-joint gig near Greenville. They played *Smokestack Lightning* together and Wolf gave Booba the nickname 'Little Wolf'.

At Lily's Lounge he played three faster blues and then launched into the distorted note-bending introduction to *Ain't Gonna Worry about Tomorrow*, a slow blues that showcases his intense guitar style. He slid into the notes as if he was forcing the strings, fighting them to find the right sound. The guitar tone was rough-edged and jagged. He held nothing back, musically or emotionally, and his guitar-playing was invested with the soul-baring emotional honesty that is the only way he knows. He seemed incapable of keeping anything in reserve. On the faster songs he played rhythm, violently chopping off one chord and launching into the next one. The stinging, ringing riffs emerged as though battered and bruised from the battle he was having against the guitar. He sang strongly and confidently with a heavy, practised voice, powerful enough to carry over the sound of the band and expressive enough not to be overshadowed by his guitar-playing.

Club and juke-joint audiences in the Delta, however, are spoiled by numerous professional, authentic, and highly skilled blues musicians. Something extra is needed if an artist is to lift himself to the next rung on the blues ladder. Booba Barnes had attempted to take this step by developing a very energetic stage act to add to his musical skills. In his younger days he used to swing from the rafters in the middle of harmonica solos. As a guitarist that is not really possible so he contents himself with a gamut of other tricks – doing the duckwalk like Charley Patton (or Chuck Berry), playing behind his head like T-Bone Walker, on his back like Howlin' Wolf, and even with his teeth like Jimi Hendrix. And all this without missing a note.

Booba's trickery certainly had the desired effect on the audience at Lily's Lounge. The joint was jumping: the dancing was fervid now and getting very frisky. Of the dancers two particular girls became the main focus of attention. One was plump with a short, tight dress and a coarse, undistinguished face. The other girl was slimmer, skinny even, and was wearing an even tighter blue skirt. She was bony but pretty with the awkwardness of youth. They reserved their sexiest, most uninhibited dancing for us, dragging us onto the floor with a swing of their sinuous hips. I imagine that we danced the boogaloo, the shuffle, and the slow drag – the steps remembered imperfectly from blues lyrics – but I have no idea if that's what they were. The best was a mid-tempo grinding dance – a dragging shuffle

Booba launches into another of those solos.
Tim Spencer

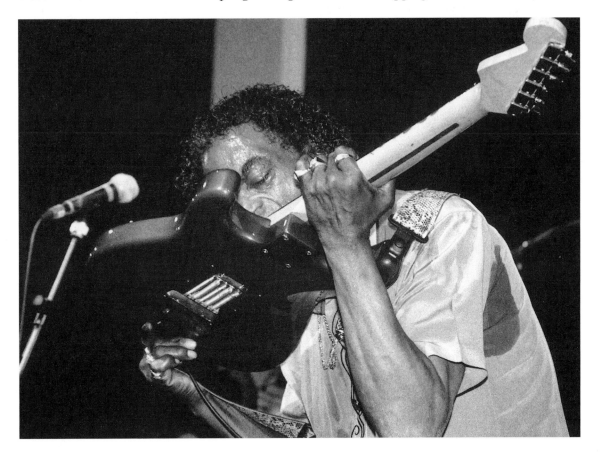

across the floor, with knees bent and legs intertwined, and the girl's hips held closely from behind.

Such explicit sexuality has been part and parcel of blues since it started. Blues has always been, in part at least, about making it, trying to make it, pretending to make it, or even faking it. 'Boogie-woogie' was slang for sex before it was a piano rhythm and 'rock 'n' roll' meant something similar before Alan Freed applied it to the country/rhythm and blues crossover music that Elvis, Jerry Lee Lewis, and Bill Haley were making. Sex has always been central to the blues both lyrically and, more importantly in this case, rhythmically.

I remembered that, back home in Britain, the Canvey Island R&B band Dr Feelgood made much of this association in their live shows. I saw them rouse a crowd to fever pitch with a particular trick that was usually done in the guitar solo during *Shotgun Blues*. Their singer, the late Lee Brilleaux, shook up a beer bottle like a victorious racing driver with a bottle of champagne. But then he made it an explicitly sexual act – holding the frothing bottle at his crotch just as the guitarist reached the orgasmic climax of his solo. The mainly male audience at their gigs lapped this up, pogoing and air-guitaring furiously as the beer bottle sprayed over them. In comparison with Lily's sexy dancers this seemed a bit tame – like a dirty old man sitting in the back row of a seedy cinema with his raincoat on.

At Lily's Lounge the sensuality of the dancing was a shared experience. Musicians, dancers, and the rest of the audience revelled in the emotions aroused by Booba's music. Two hours later, I think, the show had ended and he sat down at a nearby table and prepared to receive the congratulations and 'thank-yous'.

We had a brief conversation and I promised to come and see him if he ever got to Britain. Then I said, 'Hey man, can you do us a favour?'

'What's that?' said Booba. He was thinking, "Favour?" What could these guys want me do for them?'

'Walk us back to our car.'

'Of course, yeah.' Now he understood. 'Sure man. I'd be glad to.'

'Man, we're the only white folks here.'

That wasn't true, but it would feel like it when we got outside. Booba was only too pleased to help. They knew him out on the street. He's still a big cat in Greenville, the bluesman who went and made it big in Chicago, and he would look after us.

'It'll be all right on the street out there now. It won't be like yesterday when that guy got shot. But some of these dudes are still crazy, you know. They kill their own colour so you don't know what they might do to somebody else. That's all those mothers know. It's pitiful. I always like to treat people right. I don't care a damn what colour they are.'

Booba came to the UK year later. He was the headline act at the Gloucester Blues Festival and also played a gig at the 100 Club in London. The hall in Gloucester was cavernous, a venue more suitable for a church fête than a blues gig, but he was sympathetically backed by a British band and put on a good show. Many of the British bands who make up the bulk of the bill at these festivals are restrained and respectful in their love of blues and it sometimes shows in their performances. Their kind of faithful but reverential renditions of the blues are pleasurable in their own right but they're a long way from the guitar antics and impassioned soul-searching that Booba went in for. The audience responded to Booba like meat-eaters who had been eating tofu for too long: he was enthusiastically received.

The suit he wore on stage was, if anything, more extravagant than the one he had worn at Lily's Lounge. It certainly stood out against the 'smart but casual' garb of the band. He even did a Madonna-style costume change between the two sets and appeared in yet another outfit. He was even leaner than he had been in Greenville – I should have realized that this thinness, which I had taken as a healthy sign, could just as easily have been a sign of ill health. His sunken cheeks and thin face emphasized the distinctive stare of his bulging eyes.

He held nothing back in performance and used all his favourite guitar player's tricks. It was a passionate performance, and he attacked the songs with an almost desperate vigour. Months later I was to realize that he probably was desperate. At the end of the performance he took the opportunity to make an affectionate and rather tender little speech to his girlfriend, who was standing backstage watching the performance.

I spoke to him afterwards and reminded him about the night in Greenville. He remembered it almost as clearly as I did. Nelson Street was even worse now, he said, and he had not been back there to play.

A few months later I heard that Booba had died, struck down just as he found a new level of stability in his career and a new happiness in the relationship that he had celebrated so publicly at the Gloucester Festival. The cause of death was the subject of vague rumours, rumours that mentioned the same 'debilitating viral condition' that has been the cause of death of so many actors, fashion gurus, and ballet stars.

4 HOG'S-HEAD BLUES IN BENTONIA

JACK OWENS AND BENTONIA BLUES

'THAT'S HIM, THAT'S JACK. I'm sure that's his old truck.'

The beat-up pick-up truck had passed us going the other way, towards Bentonia, Mississippi, where we had just come from. The old man driving it was tiny and hunched over the big steering wheel.

'Quick. Turn round then!'

'We gotta turn round here and catch him up.'

We had come all this way – we didn't want to miss him. A quick U-turn in a big VW van on a tiny, Delta dirt track with big ditches on either side was never going to be easy. Especially when we had already driven miles into the depths of Mississippi to see the legendary Jack Owens and had to be quick or we would miss him. The VW ended up in the ditch with the back wheels spinning uselessly. It was a blisteringly hot afternoon, too hot to be in a van without air-conditioning, definitely too hot to be trying to push it out of a ditch.

'I'll walk to those houses and try to call someone for some help. Maybe they've got a truck, they can pull us out,' I volunteered.

Most of the houses looked very empty, doors firmly closed, curtains tightly drawn. No one came to the door when I knocked. Finally a curtain flicked and a woman's face peered out.

'Yes?' She was suspicious and uncertain. A stranger, on foot and knocking on doors during the hottest part of the day, was a great rarity.

'We're stuck in the ditch about a mile up the road. D'you think I could use your phone to call a tow-truck?'

'My husband ain't here. I don't wanna let you in.'

We really were up-country here. Her watchfulness was not surprising – strangers probably bring nothing but trouble.

'Maybe you know a garage near by . . . you know, where they have a tow-truck that could come and pull us out?'

Jack Owens
on his front
porch.

'I don't know. Lemme go look.'

I thought she was never coming back. The sun burned the back of my neck. I swatted a fly away. A full ten minutes later she came back to the gap in the curtain.

'I've called them. They'll be here in an hour. The man says it'll cost you $40.'

'Thank you, ma'am. Thank you for your help.'

I went back to the van. We were saved a hot wait because a neighbour had come by in his pick-up truck and pulled it out. So at last we found Jack back at his house, looking cool and comfortable on the porch.

'It'll be all right to sit on the porch – I thought the sun was too hot,' he said after we had introduced ourselves. 'None of y'alls from round here, are you?'

'No. I'm from London. Logan and Halle are from Memphis.'

'Is that so?'

Jack Owens was a fine-looking man, in a way that really only old men can be – he had a settled look, as though he had made a certain peace with himself and the world. He had a gentle, serious face, lit up by his gold-toothed smile.

Jack's old friend, Son Thomas, had already prepared me for the Jack Owens smile: 'He's got some pretty gold in his mouth . . . every time he would open his mouth to sing that gold would shine in the sun and the girls would scream.' Jack was also a bit of dandy: he wore sturdy leather brogues, a tight, neat waistcoat, and a cap festooned with badges, buttons, and studs. He wore belt and braces, the belt a leather number with a chunky metal buckle.

We knew that Jack was old but had never been able to work out how old: 'You're over 80 now, aren't you, Jack?'

'Yes, sir . . . I'm 87 now . . . that's what they say.'

'When's your birthday?'

'I don't know exactly – I think I was born in 1904. Seventeenth November, they tell me.'

■

Jack Owens was part of one of blues music's strangest traditions. Blues is usually a synthesis of earlier styles and music, captured either live or recorded at a particular stage of this development. Thus, Robert Johnson adapted the Delta standard *Rolling and Tumbling* and recorded it as *If I Had Possession Over Judgement Day*. Muddy Waters turned *Catfish Blues* into two songs when he recorded for Chess: *Rolling Stone* and *Still a Fool*. Each artist has adapted and developed the songs and styles of their heroes and predecessors. The blues that Jack Owens played was different – it had remained largely unchanged for decades, preserved in the spooky, remote countryside around Jack's home town of Bentonia, Mississippi. Few played

quite like him and even fewer followed him. Skip James was the best-known bluesman of this style (sometimes called 'The Bentonia School') and many of the songs that Jack played were also played and recorded by Skip. The most famous are *The Devil* or *Devil Got My Woman*, as it is sometimes called, and *Hard Times* or *Hard Time Killin' Floor Blues*.

Jack Owens
at home.

The Bentonia guitar style sounds strange to anyone used to the electric blues of Chicago or the raw and strongly rhythmic Delta guitar style. It is played on acoustic guitar, the strings being plucked, not with a plectrum but with finger and thumb picks or with specially grown fingernails. It is an eerie, gentle sound, with intricately picked runs and flurries on the guitar. Somehow it can convey a deep sense of menace and also a haunting delicacy. There is no strict 12-bar, AAB blues format. The Bentonia blues is more fluid and the sung lines are often repeated several times, and may meander from one theme to another. Usually these themes are dark and often supernatural: death, loneliness, and evil are the favoured subjects. It is an arresting, complex sound that repays careful and repeated listening.

'So you used to play with Skip James, Jack?'

'Yes, sir. I learned him a whole lot.'

'*You* taught *him*?'

'I did.'

'Did you write your own songs?'

'I can't write.'

Jack Owens and
Bud Spires
concocting their
brand of
Bentonia blues
hypnosis.

'But did you make them up – your own words?'

'Yeah. Me and Skippy James. I learned Skippy James.'

'So he got his songs from you?'

'Yes. He got 'em from me.'

Skip James almost certainly learned much of his style and repertoire from another Bentonia guitarist, Henry Stuckey, who was James' senior by five years. More than likely Jack did too, as Skip was only a couple of years older than Jack. Skip died in 1969 so there's no one around to dispute Jack's claim that it was he who taught Skip, and not the other way around. The singing style that comes out of Bentonia is also unusual: a high-pitched moan that cries out from some distant era, haunting us with its tales of the supernatural. It is singing that conjures up ghosts and gremlins, spirits of the occult from a time when the night was dark and full of evil. When Jack sang, 'It must have been the Devil that changed that woman's mind,' the Devil momentarily becomes a reality – the disbelief of a late-twentieth-century agnostic suspended for a terrifying, brief moment by the plausibility of Jack's singing.

Jack was a farmer for decades, working on a small farm and playing blues in the evenings or at weekends for years before he got a chance to record. He worked for a man he remembered fondly as 'Mr Bill':

'I had nine cows in his pasture and he wouldn't charge me nothing to put them in there and every time I worked on the pasture he would pay me. "I owe you something, Mr Bill?" "No, you don't owe me a damn thing, Jack." And I said, "Well, I'm going to work on the farm" and he said he'd pay me for every day I worked and he paid me $15 a day and sometimes I'd go way out over by Bentonia and I'd have to quit at four so I could get back over the creek there and he'd still pay me the $15. He was a good fella. He had 14 tractors running and 300 hands. I hated it when he passed, he was a good fellow. I sure did. I had to move over here then.'

Jack used to run a small juke-joint which opened on Friday, Saturday, and Sunday nights. He played there with Bud Spires, the harmonica player who became his musical partner. They also played at house parties, wedding receptions, and country picnics. They were all wild affairs:

'We played all of the night. I believe it was till about 12 or 1 o'clock. No, more than that. It was along about 2 o'clock when we quit. Them white people danced all around in the house and I got half high! Feel good, mister! There was the boss man in the house and I was talking, you know, and they were in that room and they had a thing in there but I didn't know what they called it. You know it talks, a big talking machine. I say to Bud, I say, "This man here, do you know about him?" He say, "No, I don't know about him." I say, "This son of a bitch got more money than anybody in town." And we went in there on that thing. Then we kept on playing, kept on playing, played, played, and played until it was time to quit and he said, "Well, what do you all want? Do you want some meat?" So I say, "Yes, I want some meat to carry to my wife 'cos she's sick." So he took a knife and cut us some beef. I didn't want no more whisky, I'd had enough whisky and Bud got a pint of whisky. He say, "Do y'all want to hear how you sound playing?" Bud say, "Yes sir," so he started that thing off and it played and played and after a while the thing said . . . well, it was what I said, "Bud, do you want to hear about this man, do you want to know about this man?" He say, "Yeah!" I say, "He's the biggest son of a bitch in town!" That man right there! I could have went under the floor. I didn't know he heard it. I thought he would be mad but he didn't do nothing but laugh. But I was still kinda ashamed, you know, that I could drink and talk too much.'

Our conversation with Jack was friendly and relaxed. He was a gentleman and he was brought up in another era, so his 'sirs' and 'ma'ams' to us were rather discomforting. We were interrupted by the telephone.

'That's Bud, he's coming right over.'

'How old is Bud?'

'He's about sixty years old. He claims he's forty, but he's a bit more than that.'

'Have y'all been playing together a long time?'

'About twenty-five years.'

'If he was only forty, he must have been very young when he started playing with you.'

'Well, yeah, he was kinda young. He could see when we started playing together but he can't see now. He sure can't.'

'How did he go blind?'

'Well, he was putting out some of that – what's it called? – you know, on the tractors, some poison and some got in his eyes. It got in his eyes and he did never get it fixed.'

'The poison they put on the cotton?'

'Yep. The poison from the tractor, you know. You're supposed to wear some glasses when you're working on a tractor.'

'Do all your neighbours think it's strange that you have all these visitors taking pictures of you?'

'Oh, yes. They come here by the drove sometimes. Sometimes I have to play for three of them and one take pictures and then another take over. And they're here taking pictures every which way.'

'And what do your neighbours think of that?'

'They say I oughtn't to have people like that round here and I say, "Well, if I'm going to make any money . . ." Yeah, they been here from England and from all over there, right here.'

'Well, they've probably heard your records over in England.'

'They got plenty of them over there. The sent me a letter saying I sold so many records and they wasn't paying me right and I got to get me a lawyer.'

'But they do pay you, don't they?'

'They pay me but they wrote me a letter saying they weren't paying me right, and I should leave it to a lawyer.'

'Did the lawyer get you some money?'

'I ain't never getted it.'

Jack stood up and went into the house. He was looking for a tape that he had made. 'I got a record here somewhere. I made my own record. When they stole into my house, they stole all my records. They stole I don't know how many records I had here. They stole 'em all.'

'From this house?'

'Yes, sir. From this house. The fellow was from over Chicago or England – somewhere back out over there. I gotta make me one record. He put three records on one piece. That's the only record I got to play now. I've made some nice ones but folks just stole them all.'

'But they didn't steal your guitar?'

'No, that's true. They don't bother with the guitar.'

Jack's ragged-looking but friendly dog bounced over to get some of its master's attention.

'Doesn't he guard your house?'

'He let me know when somebody pass at night.'

'But he didn't stop them stealing your records?'

'No, he didn't stop them. He's tired, you know. Yes, he'll whup any other dog. If he see me get in the truck, he'll jump in there. If I'm driving along the road and them eight dogs follow me over the bridge, he jump out and whup them eight dogs.'

'All eight of them?'

'Yes, sir. They run away from him and then he climb back in this truck.'

'Is that your truck as well?'

'Yes, sir. I won that old car there, you know.'

'You won it?'

'Yes. Playing the guitar. That was last year. A fellow told me to come down and play with him and he said he'd whup me but I beat him. He was from somewhere out around Jackson, I can't think of his name. He was drinking in there and I beat him playing and he said, "Well, you got your car," and I got it and came on home.'

'And he gave you the car without argument?'

'Didn't talk at all. Just said, "Get your car, you've got it." Got the title in the back of the car. A fellow wanted to buy the car, well, he wanted to buy the motor out of it. I tell him I'd sell the car but I don't want to sell the motor. It had a good motor in it too. He just wanted the motor. He had a pretty car too. That motor would have fit his car.'

'Does it still work?'

'Yes. It still work – it's just the battery's dead. Maybe some gas and then it'd be all right. It's a good old car too. It'll haul you anywhere you want to go. We ought to go back there and open the gate – they ought to be here soon.'

'It's all right. The gate's open. So where are you playing next?'

'We s'posed to go across the sea this month. This month just come in, ain't it? Yes, we're supposed to go across the sea sometime this month but I ain't much particular about going.'

'I think you should go.'

'Yes, but them airplanes are falling so fast . . . there's been three just this last week.'

'They're very safe. Fewer people die in airplanes than they do in cars.'

'I'm scared to get on but if I get drunk before . . .'

'Folks in England would like to see you play.'

'Yes, that's true 'cos a whole lot of them have been here. They've been coming here for something like eight years . . .'

A car drew up outside Jack's gate. The driver got out and came towards the gate.

'Ah, here they are now,' said Jack, who was looking forward to Bud's arrival.

The fingers that made it all happen.

Jack led Bud up onto the porch like a devoted grandson taking his grandfather for a walk, except the ages are reversed – Bud is in his sixties, much younger than Jack. He's also argumentative and provocative: 'You don't need to say "sir" all the time, Jack.'

Jack says he can't help it, it's just the way he was brought up: 'When I was a boy, if you didn't say "sir" and "ma'am" to white folks they'd take you away and kick you into a ditch.'

We asked Jack to call us by our names.

The autumn sunshine was cooler now and we were enjoying the calm of this strange, separated place and of Jack and Bud's by-play.

'That's good.' Bud took a gulp from his gin.

'What kinda harp have you got? Same one?' Jack said. He was getting ready to play now.

'Same one. If I change this, you gotta change guitar with me.'

Jack went back into the house to find his picks and another bottle of gin. He was sure that he had a special bottle with a hog's head on the label. None of us knew a brand with a label like that. We didn't really believe him.

Jack was looking outside in his garden, and in some boxes at the side of his house. The dog yapped at his heels and chased its tail. Jack described the label again: 'It's got a head on it and the teeth with his mouth wide open.'

'There ain't no bottle with a hog's head on it.' Bud took another gulp from his bottle. 'I don't care whether it's got a hog's mouth or a mule's mouth.'

Jack emerged from the woodpile with his dog and beamed his golden smile. He held up the bottle – Gordon's Gin, from England – the yellow and red label with the hog's head on it was unmistakeable. The dog barked again and leapt up to lick Jack's hand. Bud just took another gulp from his bottle. 'You like that gin you got there, don't you Bud?'

'Yeah. I ain't choicy. I don't care if it has a hog's head or not. It can have a mule head on it if you want. I'll tell you all a good joke.' He held up his gin: 'This stuff here can make you feel rich when you ain't got nothing in your pocket. One time two hoboes – do you know what a hobo is? – they found some of that old whisky. Corn whisky. They bottled up some and put it down by the side of the railroad. "Hey, John." "What?" "I see some water." They spotted that white lightning. So they said, "Yeah, Bob, yeah we pour some now." He said, "Take some water," 'cos it's white, you know, like water. He said, "This ain't no water. It's firewater." So they drank some. I don't know if you all drink or not but I've been that way too when you drink so much you got nothing left in the bottle but you feel rich. So they sat down by the railroad.'

'Don't get drunk now, Bud!' Jack piped up from inside the house. He was on another search mission, this time for his guitar.

Bud turned back to us: 'I don't get drunk, he's just finding his guitar, old grandpa. So they have another taste of that quart of white lightning. "How do you feel, John?" "I feel good now." "Get you another drink John." So he got another drink and knocked that quart about half way. Boy, he was all right then. Rich and everything then. So there they are, two old hoboes sitting on the railroad. One old hobo leaned on the other. "What you leaning on me for?" "I feeling good now. You know what, John?" "What?" "I'm going to buy me a damn railroad." He rich now sitting down there on the railroad. They ain't got a damn dime but they feeling rich. "Yeah, I'm going to buy me a railroad. What you going to do?" The other hobo said: "How you going to buy a railroad?" "I'm going to buy it." "No you ain't." "Why not, why can't I buy no railroad?" "Because I ain't going to sell it to you!" He's rich you see, railroad-owning him. See that's how you feel. You drink and you're rich then. One wants to buy it and the other won't sell it. There they are sitting down on it!'

They were ready to play but Bud wanted to sort out money first. He made sure that no one took advantage of Jack and his good nature. It was a symbiotic relationship – Jack was Bud's eyes and Bud was Jack's bookkeeper, his debt collector, and even his booking agent.

'Are you all going to pay me?'

'Yes.'

'I think Jack's lost his guitar. Jack! Do you have it? He's going to play soon. It's not going to take him long to tune up. This here case for my harp is all broken.' He shook his harp, banging it against the palm of his hand. 'Jack. You might need to put a little water in this thing. You got some water?' Jack came out with a gin bottle and his guitar and poured the water from the bottle.

'What's the water do for it? Do you drop it in water?'

'Open the keys up. You know like I blow it and it sticks. You just pour it through them keys. Pour some firewater in it and then I'll blow some shit!'

'Are you pouring gin in there?'

'No. It's water. Pour some gin in there and it'll blow itself!'

Jack pressed multi-coloured picks onto his long, slight fingers. They looked very tight.

■

Jack played a 12-string guitar but with it strung with only six strings. He was not far short of ninety years old when we heard him playing and, unsurprisingly, his playing and singing had lost some of their fluency. Both improved as he warmed up but his age meant that it took him longer to really feel the blues he was singing. At its best, however, his music still had a unique power to fire the imagination. The mournful singing managed to convey the history and suffering of scores of generations like a musical history book except that it spoke more clearly, more vividly, of hardships, deprivation, and human suffering than any work of social history. Jack never merely paid lip service to the dark, deep themes of the Devil, sin, and evil that he sang about and, as he warmed up, the impact of his singing increased and each successive line had a cumulative, hypnotic affect that transported you to another time and another place, to a world where the daily concerns of life were no longer love, money, and jobs but evil spirits and the Devil's temptations.

> Nothing but the Devil, baby, changed that good woman's mind,
> Nothing but the Devil changed that woman's mind,
> Devil got religion, what you say,
> Devil got religion and joined the Baptist church.

The sun had dipped down behind the trees when Jack and Bud finished playing. Jack's fingers were swelling up and his voice needed a break; Bud just needed to rest. We thanked Jack, said goodbye, and helped Bud into the van. His house was not far away as the crow flies, just over the creek at the back of Jack's house; but along the twisting little roads in that part of Mississippi, at night with a blind man as a guide . . . I had a quiet word with Jack, who confirmed that we would have no problem finding our way. Bud knew the road 'like the veins on his hand'; he would be able to direct us and the dark made no difference to him anyway.

We settled Bud into one of the comfortable back seats of the van, gin bottle in one hand and cigarette in the other.

'Did we go over the railroad tracks yet?' he asked when we had been driving for 15 minutes.

'No, I didn't see them.'

'I didn't feel them. The grocery store, did you see that?'

'No, Bud, I haven't seen that either.'

We doubled back and forth, trying to pick up the right road. Bud was silent now, removed from the cosy familiarity of the places and people he was used to. We eventually found someone who knew where Bud lived. We saw him safely to his front door and wondered how we would find our way out of this Bentonia maze.

Jack and Bud continued to play regularly at blues festivals. I saw Jack entrance a properly respectful audience at the King Biscuit Blues Festival in the late summer of 1995 when he was 90. Sadly, Jack Owens died in February 1997.

5 *D*ON'T CALL ME NO NIGGER

SCOTT DUNBAR AND SON THOMAS

MISSISSIPPI BLUES ARTISTS mine many different seams of the blues tradition. The contemporary artists make records and tour, updating the traditional sounds and adding their own more modern interpretations. Jack Johnson (see Chapter 10) is now a full-time musician with a record deal up in Chicago. R.L. Burnside and Junior Kimborough (see Chapter 13) take their own blues versions of contemporary dance music to festivals and clubs in the North as well as the South and even to Europe, and the scene in Clarksdale is alive and well, if not as extensive as Chicago's.

There are other traditional blues artists, however, who survive in a wholly different world. They make occasional records on small local labels, they put in regular but poorly paid festival appearances in the Delta every summer, and play at other more frequent local gigs for the rest of the year. And that's it. Sometimes wider recognition comes through a track on a compilation album or 'rediscovery' by a blues writer or musicologist. Since Alan Lomax in the 1940s and Sam Charters in the 1950s, blues experts have come into the Delta, seeking their own personal undiscovered stars – unknown country blues artists, the last survivors of an old tradition.

James 'Son' Thomas and Scott Dunbar fall into this second category. They were both old-school musicians who gained only marginal and belated outside recognition for their music but who nevertheless deserve some posthumous acknowledgment of the vitality of their personalities and the honesty of their skills. Both have died in recent years and both were representatives of a blues tradition at a particular time – snapshots, if you like, of the music's past. They did not update like Big Jack or even Booba Barnes but they kept alive older, pre-war blues styles.

When we met them, they were both old men though their ages were over twenty years apart. Scott Dunbar was old in years, nearer ninety than

Son Thomas at
the Delta Blues
Festival in
Greenville.

eighty but James 'Son' Thomas was only in his mid-sixties – it was illness and hardship that had aged him prematurely. Their musical voices were dimmed and their visions blurred but the skills and passions that had sustained them were still discernible. The enduring dignity of these two old men spoke volumes for the indomitability of their spirits in the face of all the hardships – physical and mental – that life had thrown at them.

■

Scott Dunbar never really gained any recognition outside a specialized community of blues aficionados – his talent was not innovative or unique enough to impose itself on a wider audience, nor did he have the craving for fame or recognition that might have enabled him to overcome this handicap. In short, he got what he wanted out of his musical ability, out of the music itself, out of *his* blues, because he did not need the wider popularity that some artists crave.

He was born in 1904, near Lake Mary, a horseshoe-shaped river cut-off in southern Mississippi. He lived there for most of his life, eking out a meagre but sufficient living as a fisherman and river guide. He was also a farmer. He started young, when he was barely old enough to walk to the cotton fields. 'My daddy carried me into the field to chop cotton,' he recalled.

There was no time for a conventional school education and he never had enough schooling to learn to read and write properly. But he loved the riverside life and was as comfortable in and on the water as he was on dry land, taking people out in his boat, catching a few fish, fixing an outboard, maybe larking around in the water and playing a little guitar in the evening.

'The water used to come up so high I could step out of bed into the water,' he remembered. 'I been fishing since I was a little boy, ten years old. I was a champion at fishing with two hooks. I once caught a white catfish so big you couldn't pick him up. You gotta stand on the bank and throw the hook into the current. I could swim a mile and I bet old Daddy Austin, an old one-eyed fellow, $100 that I could do it. I tread water like I'm walking, if you stop treading water your nose go under and you strangled by water. I grabbed a alligator gar between my legs and he pulled me so fast my back was up in the air. That gar carried me so fast like an airplane. I thought that gar was going to get me, but I won that $100!'

Scott painted an idyllic picture of his rural life: fishing, swimming, farming, and guitar-playing. He was a crack shot too, and used to shoot birds with a 16-gauge shotgun for $10 bets. 'I got me a lot of $10 like that.'

This youthfully enthusiastic reminiscing set the tone for our interview with Scott. Despite his age – he was 88 two weeks before the interview – he looked boyish when we met him. He was a tiny man, with skinny arms and a small, pointed head. His most noticeable feature was a pair of gnome-like

OPPOSITE:
Scott Dunbar,
happy and
contented on
his front porch.

ears which gave his face the look of a mischievous pixie. He wore a small cowboy hat with a blue bow tied around it. 'I keep this on all the time, I sleep in it if I can,' he said, 'because when I put a cap on I look like a monkey!' His gnome look was completed by trousers tucked into socks, a stubbly beard and moustache, and a constant, toothless smile.

He lived near Woodville, about fifteen miles from Lake Mary, in a small house up the road from his daughter and grandchildren. The house was sparse and immaculate, a freshly scrubbed stove in the front room and a 1980 calendar on the wall (we visited Scott in 1992). Against the wall was a clothes line with Scott's clean and ready-to-wear shirts suspended from it on metal coathangers. In one corner stood an old-fashioned wheelchair covered in a sheet – it was hidden but not so well hidden that it could not be an occasional reminder of someone gone but not forgotten. While we talked to him, cats gathered around, some of them huge and possum-like. Scott said he had 20 cats, 'I feed them all.'

■

When his daddy took him out to chop cotton, Scott was already playing guitar – he first performed to an audience when he was only eight. He learned on a small wooden guitar, home-made from a cigar box, with screws to tighten and tune the strings. 'It was made like a fiddle,' he said.

He put a band together – they played at local dances, house parties, and juke-joints, although he also remembered them going as far away as New Orleans and Texas. Like many of the country bands of the early blues era they featured a fiddle player, Len Baker, just as Muddy Waters had done when he was recorded at the Stovall Plantation in 1941. Their repertoire included many songs that are not really blues: *Swing Low, Sweet Chariot*, *Tennessee Waltz*, and the like.

Scott played his guitar with an amplifier so that the sound could cut through the noise of the parties: 'I made it groan and wail like I had a horn, with that amplifier. You couldn't sit still when I turned it up.' The parties were usually raucous, drunken affairs. Scott claimed that when he got drunk he played with the guitar between his legs, like Lonnie Johnson, and that his band couldn't play 'once the whisky had gone'. But he never really considered himself a blues performer: 'I play anything you want, any kind of song, hymns on up.' Because he could not read, every song, every lyric, was memorized, like some vast musical library. His favourites included *Baby, Please Don't Go*, *Wish I Was a Young Bird Up in the Air*, and *That's All Right, Mama*.

His first recordings were made in 1954 for the Folkways label. Several of his songs were released on compilation albums but it was not until 1970 that he recorded an album of his own, 'From Lake Mary', which was released on the Ahura Mazda label. Scott became a favourite with the local white community and played exclusively for white audiences after he and

OPPOSITE:
'Don't call me
no nigger.'

his wife agreed that black juke-joint audiences were just too violent. His music existed within a blues tradition but included many songs that were not blues. Singing and playing guitar were, for Scott, a love, a hobby that encompassed blues, not a career that excluded everything but blues.

It was not all parties and drinking. The more worldly problems of society did impinge and Scott had cause to sing the blues when, as he told us, a local white man, a warden on the lake, took to 'visiting' his first wife: 'He broke us up, so I got rid of her – me and her couldn't get along. I took my army gun and ran him out of my house. I said, "If you're looking for trouble you better turn around and go". I clicked that gun and he ran!' This took place in the pre-civil rights era when a black man could fall foul of the law or get strung up by a lynch mob just because he didn't 'sir' and 'ma'm' to white folks.

He settled back to a quiet life of farming, fishing, and guitar-playing. He strummed and sang for local audiences, black and white, whenever he could. His part of southern Mississippi is remote and even the 'blues revival' of the 1960s – when so many Delta blues artists were rediscovered by music researchers and fêted by festival and college audiences – seemed to bypass Scott in his secluded rural retreat. Doubtless his choice of material was too eclectic, not down-home enough, to please purist blues fans anyway. But, in many ways, Scott seemed to have benefited from his isolation and his non-participation in anything as trite as a 'blues revival', almost as though the music remained his beloved hobby because he did not have to share it with a larger audience.

Many country-blues artists who found wider fame became very defensive and suspicious in the face of the exploitation and avarice of managers and concert promoters – an entirely understandable attitude, given that they were only one or two generations away from slavery. Son Thomas, for example, would never employ an agent or a manager in order to make better use of his fame because the agents during his sharecropping days had kept him and his family in a perpetual state of impoverished indebtedness. Scott had none of this unfulfilled discontent. He was filled with pride in his ability and an enduring dignity that was independent of anything as transitory as a 'blues revival'. Besides, he claimed to be 'the best in Mississippi' and did not need the 'approval of white college boys' to prove it. 'Don't call me no nigger, I'm Scott Dunbar,' he said to us and that was the dictum that enabled him to survive so happily.

Sadly, Scott wasn't able to play for us, having injured his wrist while changing a tyre on his trailer. He had a tape recording of his 'From Lake Mary' album, though, and was desperately keen for us to hear it. We followed him down the street to his daughter's house, where the tape player was. The house was unlocked so we went straight in and Scott looked for

OPPOSITE:
Scott and some
of his cats –
they were never
far away.

the tape, his flow of reminiscences unchecked. He waved his arms excitedly, holding up the battered cassette like a kid with a new toy to show off. He took out the Ice T tape in the machine and played his own music. The roughness of the playback quality could not disguise Scott's distinctive singing voice, which is high and lilting, and gently expressive – I felt a curious warm glow of satisfaction that it so clearly reflected his character. The guitar-playing was simple and rhythmic, a sound to complement his voice but not to overshadow it.

While we were listening, Scott's grandchildren came home from school. They were hip young kids, with fashionable hair and new clothes and looked plump in a healthy, well-fed way. They were completely unsurprised to see their octogenarian grandfather playing air guitar to a recording of his own music and entertaining these studious-looking strangers with his old-time stories.

■

Scott died in October 1994, unknown to mainstream blues audiences and largely forgotten. His music was really only an isolated lake outside the broad current of blues. But his kindness and warmth touched the hearts of any who met him and his lack of bitterness and enmity was inspirational. His pride was never dented: 'Don't call me no nigger, I'm Scott Dunbar.'

■

When James 'Son' Thomas played for Ronald and Nancy Reagan at a Republican Party fundraiser in 1983, Reagan was at the height of his powers as an actor. He played to perfection the part of the ever-popular leader of the strongest and wealthiest country in the world. The campaign managers of the most popular US president since Franklin Roosevelt hired Son Thomas, a locally famous but nationally little-known musician and folk artist, to be one of the attractions at a gala evening during one of Reagan's tours through the South. Son Thomas still lived in a shotgun shack in a run-down neighbourhood of Leland, a poor town in the most impoverished state of Reagan's powerful union. He was paid just $100 for his appearance at the fundraiser.

The photograph of Son with Nancy Reagan is one of several faded photos which are the only decoration in the battered wooden house where Son lived with his son, Pat, when we visited him. The house had three small rooms and, at the back, a bathroom. The front room contained no furniture, only the photos that were all Son seemed to have as mementoes of a long career which eventually saw him acclaimed as a folk artist of macabre power and a traditional bluesman of rare authenticity. There was the Reagan photo, another of Son with Muddy Waters, and an old Val Wilmer photo of him back in the 1950 or early 60s.

OPPOSITE:
Son Thomas
with the
weight of his
troubles on his
shoulders.

Behind this front room was Son's bedroom where he spent most of his time. The bed was like a child's, narrow and frail, with a bare metal frame held together with plastic electrical tape, and a thin mattress that could not hide the sagging, broken springs. It was as battered and wobbly as Son himself. Next to it was a small table overflowing with clutter: Son's .22 pistol and a box of shells; business cards; scraps of paper with phone numbers scribbled on them; a fast-food carton and an old chicken leg. The room was painted a hospital-green colour and lit by one dim, bare bulb.

Son Thomas was born in the Delta in 1926 at Eden, and he never really left. He moved in 1961 but only across the state as far as Leland and, until the late 1960s, he had never been more than 100 miles from Leland. He had a day job as a gravedigger for years, and only gave it up when ill health forced him to rely on the small income that his music and art brought in. His deep, dark, heavily emotional singing and simple, down-home guitar-playing became very popular on the blues festival circuit and Son became an ambassador for old-style, unadorned songster blues. He travelled all over the States and went to Europe several times.

He was just as well known in folk-art circles, famous mainly for his haunting clay skulls and coffins. The skulls are roughly hewn out of clay and finished with real human teeth – out of necessity, not artistic fancy: Son had tried using corn but it germinated in the damp clay and cracked the skulls. Real teeth were hard to come by so most of the clients that Son had queueing up knew obliging dentists. His skulls are rough and real, redolent of the hardship and rawness of the Delta, and the teeth give them a macabre quality, made more striking when the viewer knows that the teeth are used out of by necessity not artistic fancy. As in his blues, Son's art reflects his life and character without any intervening pretension.

■

Son looked weary, world-weary. It was shocking to me that he looked so old: he was only in his mid-sixties, after all, and Scott Dunbar, who was over twenty years older, seemed far more sprightly and less ravaged by his years. Son talked slowly and deliberately, his voice surprisingly deep for such a slight man – a symptom of the emphysema from which he suffered in the last years of his life. He certainly had more than his fair share of health problems: as well as chronic emphysema and a bad back, which forced him to give up his job as a gravedigger, he was shot in the stomach in 1981 and had a brain tumour operated on in 1991. Six weeks later he was back on stage at the Greenville Festival, singing with his shaven skull still held together with surgical staples. Son suffered other health problems. When we visited him, he had recently fallen onto his electric bar heater, an accident which had recurred several times since 1985.

'My face swelled up and I had to have an operation.'

OPPOSITE:
Son, backstage
at the
Greenville
Blues Festival.

'So did they fix you up all right in hospital?'

'They sure did . . . but the bill. They asked me one time when I got shot, they asked did it hurt? And I said, no, the bullet don't hurt but that bill sure hurt.'

'So your head doesn't hurt from the operation. It feels better, does it?'

'Well, it ain't never hurt.'

'How did you know you had to have an operation if you didn't have headaches, if it didn't hurt?'

'I didn't never had one. They got me on the machines and they taking pictures and they seen what was wrong.'

'So you had big stitches on your head?'

'The only thing that hurt me was when they stuck me with all them needles for taking blood tests.'

'Where were you in hospital?'

'In Greenville.'

'So you didn't go to Memphis?'

'No.'

'How long did you have to stay in?'

'I don't really know directly when because my mind is all messed up, but I know I got out some time around the end of August because the first blues festival is in September.'

'So you came straight out of hospital and played at the festival?'

'Yes, yes, just after coming from the hospital. I owed them people a lot of money so I had to sing. But I just quit worrying about it. They were still bugging me for the bill. There ain't telling how much money I still owe them. I quit worrying about it.'

Son said that his hospital bills came to over $50,000, but that he had no medical insurance.

'And how do you feel now?'

'My hands are slower.'

'That's from when you fell on your heater?'

'Right. It was like that one 'cept it didn't have a grate and I fell in it and burnt this hand and my leg got burnt and I stayed in hospital a long time from that.'

'Did that happen a long time ago?'

'Back in the 80s, wasn't it, Pat?'

'About '85, I think.'

Son was looking even more tired and it was catching – he was making us all yawn. An almost physical wave of depression came over me, heavy and low like an approaching storm. This talented, vital man had no energy left, no strength held in reserve to combat the difficulties that his existence continued to throw at him. He deserved more for his pains.

'Do you have any wind today? Would you mind playing a song?'

'I'll try.'

OPPOSITE:
Son, in a
typically
no-nonsense
mood at the
Greenville
Blues Festival.

He played, sounding as deliberate and slow as he had when speaking. I looked at Logan, who had introduced me to Son and was now taking photographs of him. We were both wondering how much wind Son had, how much life force he had left to fight his illnesses and injuries. His guitar-playing echoed with sounds of ancient blues and with more modern rock-based material. I regretted that I had never had the chance to hear him play when he was younger and healthier, at the peak of his powers.

As a blues singer and guitarist, he was not original but he sang and played with a down-to-earth rawness that was a throwback to an earlier blues age of dances and house parties where long, extended blues were played until the dancers ran out of energy. He knew all the blues standards and sang them in a style that recalled a pre-Chicago blues era when singers roamed their communities, providing plantation workers and sharecroppers with all their fun and entertainment.

Son at home, remembering the old days.

He played some more and then retuned so that he could play slide on an old Elmore James number.

'Did you ever hear Elmore James play?'

'Oh yeah, he used to let me play his guitar. I had my own electric guitar and he had another – a smaller guitar and he had a pick-up here right over the hole.'

'So he could play it through an amplifier?'

'Yeah.'

'Where'd you run into him? At Helena?'

'Over in Yazoo County. He used to play in a club over there between Yazoo City and Eden out on Highway 49.'

His slide-playing still sounded slow and a little incoherent, soft and mushy where it should have been sharp and jagged. It picked up when he played Elmore's *Dust My Broom*.

'What does that mean: "Dust My Broom"?'

'That mean like you is on the plantation and you singing "dust my broom" just means you goin' to run off.'

'Quit work?'

'That's what "dust my broom" mean.'

Son handed the guitar to Pat, who played a few Elmore James licks while his father talked. Pat sounded unpractised and could not master the classic Elmore slide intro.

'I can't get that slide part. I can only get that first part of it. I hold my hand too stiff for one thing,' he said, acknowledging his shortcomings. Pat had played rhythm to his father's lead guitar at the Greenville Festival in 1992 but his playing was as simple that day as it was when we heard his Elmore James attempts. Since his father's death Pat's guitar-playing has undergone a Robert Johnson-like transformation. He has taken on Son's blues mantle and performed in a style similar to his father's at several blues festivals.

Pat gave up his attempts and handed the guitar back to his father. Son started to play another song, slow and sad. *After the War* was poignant with lyrics that sighed with weary resignation at the wrongs of the world. He played it like a sick old man who knew he was on his last legs. He finished playing and rested his head on top of the guitar, exhausted by what once must have invigorated him.

Son had several nicknames. He used to be called 'Cairo' after one of his most popular songs, *Cairo Blues*. 'Secretary' recalled the time, as a teenager, when he had worn glasses and kept the books of a neighbouring white family.

'Why do they call you "Son"?'

'My mother and my grandmother, they all called me 'Son' and a lot of people started calling me "Son Ford" because I used to make little Ford tractors.'

'Who taught you to play?'

'It took me three months and then I learned how to make a note from my uncle.'

'Your uncle just recently died, didn't he? What was his name?'

'Right. Joe Cook.'

'He was a blues musician?'

'Yeah.'

'You know Jack Owens, don't you?'

'I sure do. He's a real old man. I mean, I'm 65, no, I mean 66, but he was an old man when I was a boy.'

'I think he's 88 or 89 or something.'

'He's got some pretty gold in his mouth. My mother let me go down to Mississippi and Jack Owens was playing there. And every time he would open his mouth to sing that gold would shine in the sun and the girls would scream.'

'Do you like his guitar-playing?'

'Yeah, I like his guitar and his singing – them old tunes. But what they doing now they ain't playing no blues, they just playing rap music.'

'Don't you like rap?'

'No. None of them youngsters coming up now like the blues. It ain't hip now. They were hip back then.'

'Do you know Scott Dunbar?'

'I've heard his name but I don't know if I've ever met him. I seen a book of him.'

'What's that? Is that the book Bill Ferris did?'

'Yes.'

Scott is on the cover of the book, but it is Son Thomas who is its real star. It is his intimate insights and frankness that provided Ferris with most of his best material, as well as revealing the vigour and energy that Son had possessed as a younger man.

Son was dead less than a year after our interview. He suffered a stroke and a month later, on 26 June 1993, he died in hospital. As in Scott's case, Son's blues had been part of his life, not a career choice or rational decision, just one of the things he could do well, a way of coping and a means of expression that needed no further explanation or thesis to justify its position in his life.

OPPOSITE:
A proud man
and a renowned
artist.

6 | *B*REAKING DOWN THE WALLS

THE MEMPHIS BLUES SCENE

IAMOND TEETH MARY sat in her wheelchair, centre stage, brightly lit now that the house lights had come up at the end of the evening's entertainment. A burly-looking roadie, twice her size, wrestled half-heartedly to take the microphone she was holding. The annual Handy Awards ceremony, where the Oscars of the blues industry were handed out, had just finished at the New Daisy Theatre, Memphis, Tennessee. It ended with more of the controversy and bitterness that had dogged its progress for weeks. Diamond Teeth Mary was the surprise star performer of the show, winning over a hesitant audience with her versions of blues classics. From her wheelchair she dominated a stageful of blues legends in their final, encore version of *The Blues is Alright*, coaxing a standing ovation from the crowd before they left the theatre.

As they filed out, she launched into a blistering tirade against the organizers of the show, the Blues Foundation. She claimed that they had promised her so much money and still not paid her. Her stated case was that she was a 90-year-old lady who deserved better; was this any way to treat folks? Buddy Guy tried to coax the microphone off her but she would not give it up. Who did they think they were? She'd been promised an award; that was how they had persuaded her to travel hundreds of miles to be there in Memphis on a Sunday evening.

Of course she was right. To my eyes, the whole event had been an organizational shambles – albeit an enjoyable shambles. Last-minute hosts Andrew Love and Wayne Jackson seemed under-prepared and, dare I say it, they appeared to be over-imbibed. As the Memphis Horns they have, of course, played with all the greats, from Otis Redding to Robert Cray, and so they carried it off with the right measures of gauche embarrassment and insouciant charm.

Buddy Guy was the last-minute star guest and he collected a total of five Handy Awards: for Contemporary Album, Song, Guitarist, Vocalist, and

Diamond Teeth
Mary, centre
stage at the
Handy Awards.

Buddy Guy collecting one of his Handy Awards.

Entertainer of the Year. The Foundation had no money to pay any of the artists and Buddy had only been called up at the last minute. He wasn't going to play, though, because they wouldn't pay for his band to come down from Chicago and a man of Buddy Guy's status and with his pride wasn't going to play with a pick-up band. That was an indignity that dated back to the days when the white promoters and record-label owners wielded their financial clout like eighteenth-century plantation owners. As usual, Buddy wore dungarees, a dignified man full of pride in his background and upbringing. In his own words: 'You can take the man out of the country, but you can't take the country out of the man.' He should have been given the chance to grace the stage with his skill. Instead he sat there at a table overloaded with his awards and smiled modestly while several inferior bar-bands indulged themselves histrionically.

Amongst what I feel was the mediocrity there were musical highlights: Jimmie Rogers was traditional Chicago blues at its most concise; Katie Webster, 'The Swamp Boogie Queen', wowed us with her piano antics, wearing a huge circular hat and white, elbow-length gloves throughout her set; and, of course, there was Diamond Teeth Mary with her *Let the Good Times Roll* and *The Blues is Alright*.

It was certainly a strange crowd for a Memphis blues gathering – unusually white and unusually old. They chit-chatted throughout and the music might as well have been background entertainment at their latest charity dance or garden party. Where were the hard-core fans, the white kids in their 'Delta Blues Festival, 1990' T-shirts or the black, middle-aged city slickers with shiny suits and processed hair? Not here, with the tickets at $50 a piece. They were probably in a club somewhere watching a better band for a tenth of that price. Instead it was society fatcats in sports jackets and plump hostesses in cocktail dresses, flashing their stuffed wallets and expensive jewellery.

What rankled most with me was not the average quality of some of the acts, the ramshackle charm of the evening's progress, or even what seemed to be the uninterested ignorance of the audience, but the sour taste of exploitation that hung over the auditorium like CS gas. It seemed that this was not a celebration of blues and its musicians, a reward for a year's hard work. Instead it appeared for all the world like a society jamboree in which the elected and self-appointed big-shots of Memphis assumed ownership of the grass-roots music that they have consistently ignored for so many years.

What should have been the blues gathering of the year, with local and national musicians celebrated and fêted, seemed to have been usurped for their own self-aggrandisement by certain locals – another entry in the résumé, another charity patronized. Most of the city's indigenous musicians were ignored when the bill for the show's music was drawn up and those from the rest of the country, like Diamond Teeth Mary, were treated with scant respect. In a demonstration of crass insensitivity and ignorance, half the award-winners were not even invited to the event and it looked very much as if a 90-year-old woman in a wheelchair was dragged halfway across the country under false pretences.

Memphis already had a history of slighting its musicians. In 1987 the Mayor had planned a concert to honour Martin Luther King but announced that he expected all the contributing musicians to perform for nothing.

Isaac Hayes told journalists, including *Rolling Stone*'s Stanley Booth: 'Those assholes. That's why I left Memphis. They're supposed to be statesmen and leaders and they're so ignorant. There's still bigotry. They wanted to do a concert to show how far Memphis has come, and not pay anybody. That shows exactly how far.' (*Rythm Oil*, Stanley Booth). *Plus ça change, plus c'est la même chose.*

It is the musical heritage of Memphis that has put it on the world map – say 'Memphis' to anyone around the world and they will think of Elvis and Sun Records, Beale Street and blues, Booker T. and the MGs and Al Green. It is this heritage that the city's 'leaders' continue to ignore and exploit but seldom respect or celebrate.

In the early decades of the century, Beale Street was the main entertainment street for the black population of the South. It was probably the most important centre of black popular entertainment for the whole of the United States. Audiences flocked from all around to see the greats of jazz who played at the Hippodrome or the Palace or the Lincoln theaters. You might catch Bessie Smith, Ma Rainey, Duke Ellington, or Count Basie. If it was more down-home fun you were after, there were blues in the bars and clubs up and down the street, gambling dens in dingy basements and, if you still had energy and money left, whorehouses that could help you spend both.

But the officials and leaders of this heavily segregated city looked down on all this fun and games with haughty contempt. For them it brought only shame to Memphis. They saw only that their city was 'the murder capital of the South', with 89.9 murders per 100,000 citizens in 1916, and that Beale Street was a drug- and drink-fuelled nest of sin and vice for the black part of the city's population. Mind you, the sinning and law-breaking were not all one way – in 1917 a young black man, Eli Persons, was accused of raping a young white girl. The police decided that a fair trial was too good for him so they handed him over to a vengeful, baying mob, over a thousand strong, who built a bonfire, burned him on a stake, cut out his heart, and rolled his head down Beale Street.

When plentiful jobs in northern cities like Detroit, Chicago, and St Louis drew thousands of migrants north, Memphis was the conduit through which they came. The main railroad from New Orleans and the Delta to the North was the Illinois Central, which went through Memphis, bringing with it the blues from the Delta. Mixed with the rich musical heritage of Memphis, the blues went to Chicago and the rest of the world.

In the 1940s and 50s, this musical mix was cooking. There was a new radio station, WDIA, which, in 1949, became the first all-black station. It had a huge 50,000-watt transmitter, which enabled the signal to reach right down into the Delta, and on good days into New Orleans. Rufus Thomas, a local musician and theatre performer who had been appearing on Beale Street since he was six, became the star of the revamped station, thrilling audiences with his exuberant jive talk. He was already an experienced compère, having hosted a regular talent night at the Palace Theater, and he brought his sassy street talk to a huge new audience. The station became a focus for the whole black community in Memphis and the Delta. Advertisers loved it because this was the first time they could reach such a large, relatively untapped black audience. It became an integral part of the community for its audience – if you were searching for a missing dog or a long-lost relative who'd moved up from the Delta, you would raise a hue and cry on WDIA.

The city's first permanent, professional recording studio, the Memphis Recording Service, was set up by Sam Phillips at 706 Union Avenue in 1950.

Soon he was making records there on his own label – Sun Records. Within a few years he had recorded the records by the musicians who were to change the sound of popular music for ever: Elvis Presley, B.B. King, Howlin' Wolf, Carl Perkins (his *Blue Suede Shoes* was the first single to top the R&B, pop and country charts), Jerry Lee Lewis, Johnny Cash, Rufus Thomas (who had Sun's first hit), and the Ike Turner band's incredible *Rocket 88* (the first rock 'n' roll record?). Phillips took the black blues sounds of urban Memphis and of the rural Mississippi Delta and presented them to national and international listeners just as the fledgeling teenage audience was flexing its muscles in the musical marketplace for the first time.

By the time the Memphis music mix came to the boil again, Elvis had gone to Las Vegas, Howlin' Wolf had gone to Chicago, and Ike Turner had found Tina and Phil Spector. Rufus had stayed in Memphis and, with his daughter, Carla, kick-started the record label that was to be the city's next world-wide musical export – Stax records. Stax had their first regional hit with Rufus and Carla's *'Cause I Love You* and the first national one with Carla's solo *Gee Whiz*. Many more hits followed, notably those by Otis

Jimmy Rogers, one of the stars of the Handy Awards ceremony.

Redding, Booker T. and the MGs, and Albert King. The clinical classicism of the Stax sound was to become the soundtrack to an era of violent change – civil rights, sit-ins, race riots, and finally the end to the institutionalized racism of the segregation system, a system that had operated all over the South.

But the white city fathers of Memphis seemingly had an altogether different picture of their city and why it was great. Perhaps, they had the curious idea that it was a superior, aristocratic, blue-blooded capital of the South, some sort of haven of class and culture amongst the poor white country trash. They never seemed aware that it was the black music and culture that was making their city famous and attracting fans and other musicians from around the world. So the Stax studio was bulldozed and no one bothered about Beale Street until there was tourist money to be made there. Perhaps that was why no one took the trouble to invite the hard-working blues musicians of the city to the Handy Awards?

■

Ernestine and Hazel's is a long, low club at the 'wrong' end of town. When you tell white Memphians where it is – because they don't know, of course – they raise their eyebrows and say, 'Way down there!'. It really is 'the other side of the tracks'.

There is a door at one end and a small stage at the other. Along one long side is the high bar, where Ernestine Mitchell sits on a low stool with only her greying hair sticking up above the bar. The bar is narrow but behind it there is still room for a kitchen with pots of steaming chilli, and burgers frying on a griddle. On the other side are several booths and, in between them, a few tables and chairs. Suspended low over the pool table in front of the cleared stage area at the back is what serves as the stage lighting – a blue-neon-lit King Cobra Malt Liquor advertisement.

We were there to see what we'd missed at the Handy Awards – blues played in front of an appreciative, participating crowd: good-time 'forget about work, troubles, and debts' music. We had heard that Ben Wilson, leader and guitarist of local band the Hollywood All Stars, was going to be here tonight and he knows the real Memphis music scene. He was going to show us some real blues, the sort that has had an audience in Memphis for years, and has thrived independently of the tourist tat that Beale Street is now.

Ernestine Mitchell has been running clubs in Memphis for years and her late husband, Andrew 'Sunbeam' Mitchell, ran the legendary Club Paradise, one of the great blues venues, where B.B. King was a regular star attraction during the 1950s and 60s. Between stirs of the chilli pot – 'I cooked so much chilli, I get to smelling like chilli!' – she showed us a memento from those old days, a ticket from a B.B. show in 1950-something.

'The Blues is
Alright' – the
Handy Awards
finale led by
Diamond Teeth
Mary

The band at Ernestine and Hazel's was the Blues Fenders or Benders – I never did hear which. They were a relatively little-known local band, but they were still better than the rock boys doing their blues 'n' boogie thing at the New Daisy Theater. Various guests popped up on stage to do a number or two. Marino was a singer with a big Afro and a purple jump suit and he sang a Z.Z. Hill number faithfully and tunefully. Earl Forrest is one of the original 'Beale Streeters', the generation of young musicians who came to prominence in the musical explosion of the early 1950s. He was the drummer who had backed B.B. King (and Johnny Ace) when B.B. first got a band together in Memphis. He looked restrained and proud in a brown, three-piece suit. Finally we saw Ben Wilson, who looked like the bad boy of the bunch – scuffed, black cowboy boots, low-slung jeans and a hip-swaggeringly mean guitar sound. When he played, he attacked an older, deeper blues with a fury and raucousness that none of the other guitarists have even tried to attain. He does not use a pick, but plucks with thumb and fingers, flying over the strings.

When he had finished a couple of songs, Ben came over for a chat. 'I like to get paid for playing,' he said, making it quite clear that this short guest appearance had been done for nothing. We persuaded him to take us to another club where we could hear some more blues. He was not due to play anywhere else but he knew somewhere where we could hear some good stuff.

'Just stay close and follow me. You don't wanna get lost in this neighbourhood with that car.' We obviously looked a little worried. 'Don't worry, boys, you be all right with me,' he said, showing us his pistol, which he keeps hidden under his dashboard. We followed his huge, low-slung, black coupé – a relic from the pre-oil-crisis era. He drove fast and we struggled to keep up as the coupé bounced and wallowed over the rough roads. There were potholes everywhere in that part of town, deep storm ditches ran along either side of the road, and railroad tracks criss-crossed it. We were a long way from the manicured grass verges and pristine black tarmac of white Memphis.

The club that Ben took us to looked a dirty, sorry place. Clearly there was not going to be any more music there: a few customers were loitering around the door, looking a bit the worse for wear or just frightened and shifty. Inside, someone was sweeping up some broken glass; apparently a brawl had broken out. The band had finished and gone home and everyone had been asked to leave. The club was closed but there was a group of mean-looking drunks hanging around outside, hoping for some new action or another fight.

We listened to the jukebox for a while and drank a beer. Ben knew the club owner so we talked blues and played cards while Ben tried to ignore one of the drunks who was assaulting him with the usual 'you think you're a tough, big-shot musician' type of provocative talk. A knife was drawn at one point, not to be used, but as a demonstration that its owner was ready for action. The drunk eventually left us in peace and Ben prepared to go. He promised to meet us the following week at the Club Hi-Rise where he was due to play with his own band. Then he climbed into his car and roared off, waving his pistol out of the window.

The Club Hi-Rise is a big, city-slickers' club, favoured by the wealthier black community in Memphis. It was a Saturday night and when we got there soon after eight o'clock, it was already packed, full of couples dressed in their weekend finery. There was a proper dance floor, a stage for the band, and a powerful PA system, which was pumping out funky chart songs. Plump, swanky couples sat around glass-topped tables, drinking their beers and cocktails. It looked like Ben's kind of place.

Ben's band, the Hollywood All Stars, were probably the hottest band in the city. They had been playing together for 20 years. They first came together when Leroy Hodges died in 1974. Hodges had been the leading figure on the Memphis music scene and both the Hollywood All Stars and Memphis's other stand-out band, the Fieldstones, were formed out of the musicians who had played in Hodges' band, the Funky Four (from what goes around the Memphis music grapevine there had been a lot more than four of them!).

The Allstars had a big sound, with keyboards and saxophone augmenting a rhythm section but it was Ben's guitar that was at the centre of their music. He came on-stage before the band and performed a brief but impressive warm-up – a fast Chuck Berry riff and then a lean, mean John Lee Hooker one. That was it, he stopped: warmed up, tuned, and ready to go in about three seconds. The rest of the band wandered on and joined him on-stage.

They played three sets and in all three showed their musical skill and an acute sensibility to their audience's response. They had a firm collective grasp of the dynamics of live blues: the tempo changes, instrumental shadings, and awareness of audience reaction that are necessary to sustain a good show for three sets. Ben sang most of the numbers and is a true virtuoso on guitar but his expertise was underpinned by the fluidity of the rhythm section, the catholic dexterity of 'Boogie Man' Hubbard's keyboards, and the powerful honking saxophone. Hubbard was born in Memphis but has played piano in bars from New York to New Orleans, from Texas to Chicago. He fills out the Hollywood All Stars' sound, adding a touch of New Orleans calypso, or a bit of Memphis Slim barrelhouse boogie. The band played a heavy Delta blues-grunge like *Mannish Boy* just as naturally as a sax-led T-Bone Walker shuffle and their music reflects the blues journey from Delta to Memphis, from country to city: Ben's guitar sound and vocals are often as down-home and country-fied as Muddy

Ben Wilson of
the Hollywood
All Stars: the
lean, mean
sound of a true
virtuoso.

Waters' were when he first went electric but the band's jazzy, horn-led rhythms are as slick and citified as the suited card-sharps of Beale Street.

The Saturday-night crowd at the Club Hi-Rise were certainly appreciative. They applauded Ben's nasty, chortling singing and his fat-toned guitar solos and danced passionately to the saxophone sound of the faster instrumentals. Blues audiences in Memphis have grown up expecting nothing less than the best. The Hollywood All Stars did not disappoint them.

■

Green's Lounge has been a popular black club for years but in Memphis a little segregation goes a long way and lasts a long time and it is only recently that it has gained a whole new audience by becoming the in place for the more socially aware and open-minded set of young white Memphis. On weekend nights, especially when the Fieldstones are playing, the cars parked outside reflect the mix of the audience, with big old Buicks and Chevys side by side with smaller, newer BMWs, Hondas, and shiny four-wheel drives with side stripes and bull-bars – the sort that never get further off-road than shopping-mall carparks. Most of the newer cars are usually carefully parked under street lamps in the brightest spots their nervous owners can find.

There's always a security guard on the door, an old uniformed fellow with a tightly holstered pistol and a kindly smile. He frisks everyone, but I've never seen any weapons given up. It's not really a security precaution, just a strange Memphis greeting that everyone expects.

The club is decorated with those 1970s beer ads featuring ludicrously good-looking couples who smile through their Afros and sport the widest flares this side of Haight-Ashbury. Rose Green, who runs the club, knew the Memphian friends I was with from previous visits and welcomed us all as favourite customers. The crowd was a typical Green's mix: shiny-suited black couples dressed up for their big night out, young white kids in jeans and sweatshirts, and attentive groups of older fans. There were even some 'musos' from out of town. They had come for the Handy Awards and somehow found their way to Green's.

The Fieldstones play good-time, party music of the kind that has survived in Memphis despite the comings and goings of musical styles like soul, disco, funk, and rap. They provide a soundtrack to drink, flirt, and dance to, the essential musical accompaniment to a good night out. The band was formed by drummer Joe Hicks, who played in Leroy Hodges' band, the Funky Four. Hodges asked Joe to keep the band together and when Hodges died, soon after, Joe was true to his word and formed the Fieldstones, whose original members had played with Hodges.

They play an eclectic mixture of styles. The show I saw at Green's was a blend of sounds and genres that seemed to resonate with aural ghosts of

Memphis music from the last five or six decades. I heard straight blues when they did the old Robert Johnson favourite, *Sweet Home Chicago*. It had a sparseness, a springy lightness of rhythm that sounded like Booker T. and the MGs. The guitar even sang with the bright, clear sound that Steve Cropper had on Otis Redding's version of *Rock Me Baby*. The other blues that they played came with a dash of soul seasoning: Little Milton's *Little Bluebird* was written by Stax stalwarts Isaac Hayes, Dave Porter, and Booker T. Jones, and even *Angel of Mercy*, which was made famous by blues man Albert King, was recorded during his years at Stax.

Lois Brown's bass-playing was rock solid throughout. On record and in live performance, her playing gives the Fieldstones the same beefy 'bottom' to their sound that Willie Mitchell created for Al Green's. It's a soft, weighty sound like the 'whump' of a heavy pillow, but repeated with an unswerving, steady groove. Organist Bobby Carnes embellishes the Fieldstone sound with gospel accents, echoes of church music that give the sound the same ethereal feel that Willie Mitchell gave O.V. Wright's records in the 1960s. When Bobby cut loose on *Short-Haired Woman*, the soaring organ came from the same sacred place as Al Green's preaching at the Full Gospel Tabernacle church.

The atmosphere in Green's was unlike that of any other club I've been in. It was racially mixed with apparently mutually exclusive (in a city like Memphis) elements of black and white culture represented and yet there was no tension between these two. Most music venues are racially mixed but often it is almost as if the minority was some kind of guest of the majority, invited because the majority was big enough, decent enough, to let the others be there in peace, and because it reflected well on them, on their lack of prejudice and their benevolence. At Green's there was no sense that anybody was there except on their own terms. There were no deferential guests or paternalistic hosts. Primed by the atmosphere and fired by the music, I felt the club became a world on its own, a better world where there were no Los Angeles rioting, no Serbian ethnic cleansing and no Rwandan tribal massacres.

■

The Fieldstones were well into their second set and the dance floor was swaying and throbbing. I was dragged back to cold reality when I spilt my beer on the table behind me. The beer poured to the edge and slopped over. I looked into the eyes of the man at the table, expecting the usual aggressive reaction, and preparing a placatory apology, a show of contrition.

His smile eased my concern: 'Don't worry man,' he said.

'He's always spilling his beer on people,' his girlfriend added.

The man was wearing a Kansas City Chiefs cap and didn't sound like he came from Memphis.

We introduced ourselves. I've forgotten his name and I'm sure he has forgotten mine. Sometimes names don't really seem that important.

He told me that he was very surprised to see so many white people in what was clearly a black club, 'Man, I didn't expect that down here in Memphis.' He was from Kansas City, where integration, he reckoned, had made far more progress than it had down here in the South. But he had not expected to find black folks and white folks in the same club in a city like Memphis.

I told him that I thought things might be changing and that hopefully the old days were over, and then headed for the bar to fetch another round. Fuelled by fresh quarts of beer, we compared our two countries and decided that there were still huge problems in the United States and in Britain, even in the larger, cosmopolitan cities like London and Kansas City. The barriers of suspicion and fear were so high and so hard to overcome, the weight of history so overbearing, but as the spirit of the Fieldstones' musical testifying took over in Green's that night we both fancied that our meeting of minds, our shared hopes and optimism for the future, might be a small victory in this long battle to overcome the barriers, to smash the dividing walls.

My Kansas friend grabbed me by the shoulders now as our conversation became more animated. 'We've got to break down the walls,' he kept saying, 'break down the walls, friend, break down the walls!'

I shook his hand between both mine, we drank our beer, and listened to the Fieldstones.

BLUES AT MURPHY'S BAR

ROBERT 'THE WOLFMAN' BELFOUR

ROBERT BELFOUR'S TIDY, suburban house in Memphis is a far cry from a shack in the Delta, the caricature home of a blues player. It has a small front yard and the usual assortment of household implements and garden tools lying neatly on the porch. A huge Stars and Stripes flies on his neighbour's flagpole, casting its flapping shadow over Robert's garden. Robert 'The Wolfman' Belfour is a skilled and practised guitarist but he is not yet well known even amongst the blues experts of the Memphis music scene. He still gets up early every weekday to go to the construction job he has on the outskirts of Memphis. In the evening he plays guitar at tiny bars for whatever money he can get.

Robert's home has 'a place for everything and everything in place'. All the furniture and fittings are old, worn, and soiled but neat and ordered. The living room is lit by Gothic-looking wall-lamps, the dimness of their bulbs in keeping with the decor of the room. The wallpaper is green, the same shade used in camouflage, and the rural, lakeside scene above the mantelpiece looks like one you would pick up from a roadside picture-seller. Robert sits us down and introduces us to his wife. He is still at the beginning of his career as a musician and is anxious, not just willing, to make us welcome.

His family came from rural Mississippi, farming country just south of Memphis. They were sharecroppers who farmed a small acreage of land that they leased from its owners. The sharecropping system was a harsh one. Sharecroppers were given advances, usually monthly, against their earnings from the crop, usually cotton, that they were farming. They also bought their food, equipment, and other supplies from stores run by their landlords. The essential feature of the system was that it kept the sharecropping families hopelessly indebted to their landowners. There were honest and benevolent landowners but largely the system was a kind of

Robert 'The
Wolfman'
Belfour relaxing
at home.

economic bondage – the twentieth-century extension of the nineteenth-century bondage of slavery.

Music was the main source of entertainment, as Robert Belfour recalls: 'I grew up listening to the radio. There weren't too many TVs around then. We just had one of those old battery radios I used to listen to.' His father was also a musician, 'I started playing when I was eight. It was my daddy's guitar. Back then he didn't play at clubs and things, he just played at home and parties and things. I taught myself and I couldn't hardly hold it, it was so large. I had to lay it across my lap like it was a steel guitar.' More inspiration came from the radio: 'I learned myself listening to the radio, mostly John Lee Hooker, Lightnin' Hopkins, Muddy Waters. Mostly we listen to WDIA and WVEL.'

Robert can't really understand why we are so interested in his music and where it comes from. To him it was always just part of his life.

'What is the blues to you, Robert? Can you explain it?'

He does not really understand the point of the question and hesitates, wondering what it is we are getting at: 'I don't really understand . . . It's really hard to say because you can play it but you gotta have it in here to really do it, you gotta feel it inside of you. You can learn to play it, but it ain't

'You gotta feel it inside of you.'

the same.' He presses the palm of his hand over his heart, and looks a little lost. 'Cotton picking and chopping – that's when you sing the blues –
when you're behind a plough and a mule. You gotta have a feel for what
you do. It's just a feeling you have when you are playin'. The blues ain't
nothing but some part of your life, something happening in your life . . . it's
hard to say . . . I just know what it is. You really have it in here. It's serious,
you know.'

But how does blues help? Does it release some of the tension, the hurt,
the unhappiness? Music fans often say, 'Oh, I can't listen to blues. It's so
sad. It's such down music.'

'Yes, music kinda releases your feelings. You can have a lot of pressure
on your mind or financial problems or anything and you can sit down and
play that guitar and it might ease your mind. Just like if you get a drink of
whisky, but then you ease your mind and you wake up with the same problem! I can play for five hours and I won't be tired. It's just a gift.'

We take some pictures, trying to brighten the light enough to get some
good shots. Robert fetches his guitar, plugs in, and starts to sing in that
same curious voice he has when speaking. 'The Wolfman' is a bit of a mis-
nomer as well: he does have a strong, growling voice but none of the raw
savagery of Howlin' Wolf himself and none of the sense of menace that a
growl like that should bring. Perhaps he should find a more appropriate
nickname.

Murphy's is a tiny bar in the heart of the Midtown area of Memphis, a mid-
dle-class student area. Tonight there are only 11 customers, all looking like
students in baggy T-shirts, jeans, and running shoes. Three or four of them
are shooting pool in a desultory fashion and a few more are watching. A
big TV hangs high in one corner showing yet another in a seemingly inter-
minable series of baseball games. Every so often a jukebox blares into life,
spewing out a Bon Jovi or Lynyrd Skynyrd track. We know the barman so
we say hello, buy some beers, and pick one of the many empty tables.

Robert Belfour comes onto the small stage some minutes later. He's
wearing a spotless, cream-coloured three-piece suit, a meticulously tied
red tie and highly polished shoes: his best clothes, his special-occasion
suit. He is recording himself tonight and he rigs up a small, ancient-
looking tape recorder. It has a top-loading deck and oversized buttons like
something that grandfathers have hidden in their desk drawers. He hooks
up his microphone and plugs his guitar into an old amp. He tunes up carefully. The jukebox is silent now but the TV still glares. The pool players
look up and then down again, back to their game of pool. At last Robert is
ready to go. He says 'Good evening' in that measured, dignified way of his
and starts to play *Smokestack Lightning*, a staple of blues singers in bars all
over the world.

Robert Belfour,
the family man,
on the front
porch.

He finishes the song and turns towards our booth. 'I got friends here tonight, I'd like to say hello to them.'

His friendly banter is greeted with damning and almost complete lack of interest. The pool players glance up at him, then check the scores in the baseball, before returning to their own game.

He's a good guitar player, but lacks a distinctive style or sound. His set is a typical mixture with lots of Howlin' Wolf, Muddy Waters, and other Chicago classics. The obvious songs by the obvious artists. He sings the songs with feeling and sensitivity but cannot penetrate the atmosphere of an unsympathetic venue or inspire an uninterested audience. The curious, soft growl of his voice does little to help communicate the songs to them.

During the first break we say hello to Robert and thank him. He wants to sort something out with his tape recorder so he goes back to the stage and we go up to the bar to buy him a drink.

'What's Robert drinking?' we ask.

'Oh, don't worry about him,' the barman replies with a dismissive wave, 'I give him a draught now and again. That keeps him happy.'

We insist he gives us the more expensive (and tastier) bottled beer and take it up to Robert.

The second set is better. The games of pool have all finished and a few more people listen. Robert wasn't having an easy time up on stage, though. Every time he sung that bit louder or leaned closer to the microphone, he got a jolting electric shock, not an easy thing for an inexperienced performer to overcome. He wanted one of the bar staff to come and sort out their equipment, but his signals for help met with little response.

There are dozens of blues players like Robert Belfour in Memphis and many more in cities all over the South. They make a little extra money from their music, scant return for the hard work they put in and the treatment they have to endure. Most see making a record as a first step to better gigs and greater reward – but so do most musicians anywhere, I guess.

'I love to play,' he says, 'but I wish I could do some record cutting.' He wants to learn more, to develop his skills: 'I'd like to learn how to read and write music.' But what does the future hold for him, a talented but unexceptional guitarist who doesn't have the contacts or the all-consuming desire to pursue his musical career ahead of everything else?

Eventually it is closing time and Robert has to finish. The barman makes cutting signs with his extended fingers across his throat. He turns the jukebox on, loudly, drowning out Robert's tiny amplifier and cutting him off in mid-song.

8 ***D**RUMS IS A CALLING THING*

THE FIFE AND DRUM BANDS OF MISSISSIPPI

BEFORE WE MET Napolian Strickland, I had a recurring and vivid image of him in my mind. I saw him blowing the fife and stirring up the spirits of the revellers at an outdoor country picnic in rural Mississippi. 'Polie' was leading the dancing and merrymaking like some Mississippian Pan, cavorting into the twentieth century from pre-history, an X-rated Pied Piper inspiring a glorious, wanton, hot-footed dance adventure.

Yet, when I met Napolian Strickland that afternoon at his house in Como, it was impossible to match this man – who seemed to carry his fatigue, his ennui, like a shoulder-sagging dead weight – with the sensuous dancer and musician that Alan Lomax describes in his *The Land Where The Blues Began*. For the first time a worry that had nagged at the back of my mind became real, angry and red like a rash – maybe I had arrived in the Delta too late and the flourishing, contemporary blues music that I was convinced existed really had died out. Perhaps it was only preserved in tired old men's memories. As usual the truth was more complicated, but the story of the music of the fife and drum bands of Mississippi was ultimately a sad and inevitable one.

Napolian shares his house with his mother. It was like all the others in this part of town: wooden with a small porch, and with rough grass growing up to the sagging wooden steps which lead up to the porch. The paint on the outside walls was cracked and peeling, and there were cracked windowpanes and broken tiles on the roof. Napolian's mother, clad in a polka-dot evening dress that, in another age and on another's shoulders, must have looked quite at home at a graceful cocktail party, welcomed us onto the porch and, calling over her shoulder to 'Polie', who was inside the house, she beckoned us in.

Inside, the house was just as worn out and lacked the basic facilities that most would consider necessities. We went through the front door and

came straight into the kitchen: a big, almost empty room. There seemed to be no plumbing for running water and the room was lit from the ceiling by one unshaded bulb. In the middle of it stood a 1950s-style Kelvinator washing machine, the type you fill manually by pouring buckets of water in the top. A big pail of water stood next to the machine and a chair languished in the corner. The walls were bare except for a lonely picture of John Lee Hooker, which was surrounded by square of paleness where another picture had once hung.

Napolian led us into a back room, the living room, treading carefully, and leaning heavily on his stick. 'Bring your car up here off the road. There's some crazy folk around here and they drive like crazy,' he said by way of introduction, and then he went on to warn us, in his tired, resigned way, that he wouldn't be able to blow his fife: 'I don't got no wind.'

Fife and drum music, the music that Napolian can now barely play, predates blues in Mississippi and elsewhere in the South. Fife and drum bands played long before blues was played, heard, and given a name, and even longer before it was recorded. It is a haunting, primitive proto-blues that still resonates with many rhythmic echoes of its African roots. Their music was a throwback even as it came to flourish and now it is a true anachronism, struggling to survive in a world that is destroying its natural habitat. Very few musicians still play. The three remaining stars of fife and drum music are Napolian Strickland, Othar Turner – who at nearly 90 is even older than Napolian – and Jessie Mae Hemphill, who is younger but cannot play at all now because she is half-paralysed from the stroke she has recently suffered.

The influx of slaves into the fledgeling American colonies brought with them as much of the culture of their homelands as they could. Those who survived the deadly journey across the Atlantic then had to face the repression of slavery. That so much of the culture that came over with the slaves survived is testament to the strength of the human spirit in the face of harsh ordeals.

The musical tradition survived. Music had played a vital, everyday part of life in the villages of rural West African where the slaves came from. From the grasslands of Senegambia, which bordered the Sahara, through the forests along the great curving coastland of the Gulf of Guinea and down to the villages of the Bantu people to the south of the Congo River, almost all village ceremonies and celebrations had a musical accompaniment and it was communal, participatory music-making. Everybody joined in, clapping their hands, banging drums, shaking rattles, ringing bells and plucking or blowing their string and wind instruments.

These were not the formal orchestras of the contemporary European music tradition. There were no stages, bandstands, and rows of neat chairs to divide audience from music-makers, none of the staid politeness or tea-dance etiquette that prevailed in European dance music. Instead the whole music-making process relied on interplay, with dancers and musicians arousing and inspiring one another. Rhythm instruments rang out different tempos, combining to create polyrhythmic dance beats, an African pre-Phil Spector wall of sound. This was the call that elicited response from the rest of the community – the drummers' rhythms set off the dancing, which in its turn encouraged singing, hollering, clapping, tapping, beating, and blowing, which in their turn set the percussionists off on new rhythms. It was communal, call-and-response music, a rhythmic exchange of celebratory musical motifs.

Drumming was banned in the antebellum South but the other African musical traditions survived in the form of the musical accompaniment that the slaves made for celebrations like the harvest festivals, and in secular and spiritual songs. After the Civil War (1861–5) and their emancipation, ex-slaves were still tied to the land, often the same land, by the economic servitude of the sharecropping system. But their personal and recreational

'Drums is a calling thing.'

lives were not strictly controlled, as before, and the African traditions that their ancestors had brought over were fresh enough in the collective cultural memory to form the basis for the entertainment that they made for themselves in Mississippi. They learned new instruments or adapted old ones that fitted in with the sounds of their African heritage. Thus Alan Lomax could find echoes of African lute-playing in Sid Hemphill's fiddling and traces of West African pygmy hollering in the sound of his pan-pipes. He even traced the so-called 'blue notes' – the flattened thirds, fifths, and sevenths – to the music of sub-Saharan Africa.

Military influences played their part in fashioning this fledgeling music. In the eighteenth century, blacks were only allowed to join the state militias as musicians and military marching bands were often largely made up of black musicians. Thomas Jefferson's slaves got together a fife and drum band as their part in the war effort during the War of Independence (1775–83) against the British.

The repertoires of the bands that the slaves and, later, the ex-slaves formed reflected all sides of their musical backgrounds. They performed the pre-blues music that had developed from the African music their ancestors had brought with them but also music from the European tradition. They played dance music from both heritages – staid types like the foxtrot and minuet and funkier New World dances like the samba, mambo, and the tango. Country or mountain music – fiddle tunes and jigs – formed a big part of their repertoire, and ragtime and church songs were popular with black audiences. Sid Hemphill's band could play military marching music, blues, country square dances and jigs, gospel, and popular Tin Pan Alley songs.

To this day the sound of a fife and drum band takes you back to the African roots of the music more than any other blues and is just, but barely, reminscent of blues. You can hear the influences drifting in and out like a smell wafted tantalizingly to one's nostrils on a light breeze, only to be wafted away again just as quickly. It's almost as though the music straddles the line that divides blues from its African roots; it has feet on both sides of the line. Without the atmospheric backing of the drums and separated from the contributory hollering and gyrating of the picnickers, the fife sounds thin, struggling to convey any more emotion than a ten-year-old would when playing the recorder after a couple of lessons. Certainly, when I heard Napolian and Othar playing solo at home, it sounded lost and hollow, like an orchestra without a string section or a rhythm section without a drummer.

The country picnics of Mississippi's hill country are the direct descendants of those unrestrained African celebrations. In the early days of cotton's boom period, when Mississippi was full of sharecroppers and small farmers, picnics took place almost every weekend during the summer before the cotton-harvesting season started. Nowadays they take place

OPPOSITE:
Polie warms up
the party.

several times a year, usually at a major public holiday – Labor Day and Independence Day are the most popular dates. They are family affairs and friends and relatives come down from the surrounding towns and big cities in the North to taste some of their country cousins' hospitality.

Picnics usually start with a ball game and a barbecue during the afternoon, then as dusk falls and the beer flows, the music hots up and the dancing starts. People are drawn from miles around by the sound of the drums and the smell of the barbecue and the band will delve into their full repertoire to keep the dancing going – they might play country music, jigs if they have a fiddle player, and pop songs as well as blues. The parties get pretty wild, the dancing becomes more overtly sexual, and the moonshine flows freely.

Alan Lomax, who is desevedly the most celebrated folklorist of the blues, has filmed several such picnics. At one, in 1978, he actually stopped the cameras in case the sexual nature of the dancing be misconstrued by a film audience unfamiliar with the cultural background that lay behind it. He claims that the dancing youths that he witnessed in Africa were demonstrating their potential as marriage partners and that the sexual gyrating of Mississippi country picnics was fulfilling the same function. He calls it 'Africa come to life in America'.

The simple little instrument that makes these fluting sounds is homemade and easy to make too. Napolian made a rough one for us in about fifteen minutes. You cut a length of cane: just over a foot is about right, according to Othar Turner and two feet is too long. With a red-hot poker, you burn one finger-hole through the cane and then, measuring the positions with the stretch of your fingers, you burn out the other finger-holes. Napolian marks the positions of the holes with the wetted tips of his fingers and then cuts the holes with a knife and then burns them with a poker.

'You can have five or six holes. I blow with five,' Othar told us.

Once the finger-holes are made, you heat the poker up again and burn out the joints that divide the cane. If the cane is too thick, 'you shave it to make it slick'.

The drums used to be home-made too. Sid Hemphill had a shed full of instruments when Alan Lomax visited him. He made guitars, drums, fiddles, mandolins, fifes, and pan-pipes. Some of the drums were enormous – the idea was that a drum could be heard for a mile for every inch of its diameter, although when Lomax was told this he was also informed that they could not be heard as far as they used to be because 'there's so much electric in the air'. Nowadays the drums are usually bought by mail order from companies like Ludwig.

Othar Turner is the father figure of Mississippi fife players just as Sid Hemphill was when Lomax met him. He lives out in the country some way from Como and we followed the usual circuitous route to get there. He had given us directions on the phone but somehow the roads and junctions did not much resemble his description. Off-course and lost, we sought help and got different directions from everyone we asked, all explained in Mississippi hill country accents that are even more impenetrable than the accents are in the Delta.

When we finally reached Othar's farm, he sat us under a cool tree in his yard and shooed away the chickens and geese. The farm itself is at the end of a dirt road, down a slope of trees. His yard is bounded on one side by a line of trees and a stream, and beyond that there is a field where Othar keeps his horse and a cow. The horse nuzzled through the fence to drink from the creek.

At the bottom of the yard is a pigpen where his four pigs snorted and snuffled. Geese, chickens, and dogs wandered about the yard between the piles of wood, old tyres, rusting, long-abandoned tools, and newer, still-used ones. Othar is a hoarder, a man who knows he will find a use for everything he does not throw away – even if it takes years to work out what that use is. He's an old man now but still keeps busy on the farm. He won't raise cotton now; he says he picked quite enough when he was a boy. It's not the profitable crop it used to be anyway. Instead he grows corn, peas, sweet potatoes, watermelons, okra, and tomatoes.

Othar sat down with us under the tree. He was dressed like a farmer, in blue dungarees, a plaid work shirt, boots and a Bellingsley Auction

Othar Turner demonstrating his fife technique.

Company baseball cap, and had that tough, vigorous, healthy look that people who spend much of their lives outdoors have. He was nearing ninety when we met him (in 1992) but looked twenty years younger.

He started behind a mule when he was still a child: 'I wasn't but ten or eleven years. Mamma was out ploughing with the men, and I started by pushing the plough, but she say, "Don't push, let the mule pull it" and I soon learned that.' But hours behind the mule bored him and he yearned for something more interesting to occupy his mind. It came in the shape of music.

A neighbour, whom Othar remembers as R.L. Williams, stopped by while Othar was out in the cottonfields behind the mule and said, 'Othar, this is a fife I'm blowing. I'm gonna make you one.' He came back the next day and said, 'Son, I got your fife. You gotta blow it.'

It took Othar two or three months to learn but his mother was not happy: '"You're playing that cane again! Put that thing down!" she said to me and she made me – she busted my first cane!' But Othar remembered where the holes went on his cane and soon made another one, 'If there's something you want to do and you're interested in it, you can do it.'

Othar has been playing the fife ever since. He still has his own band, The Rising Star Fife and Drum Band. His daughter, Bernice, plays the bass drum and R.L. Boyce, a stalwart of the local scene, plays snare drum. They rehearse every week and their business affairs are organized by Bernice. 'She tends to my business, because I didn't get my schooling.'

Othar's life seems well rounded – he has a family, and lives a satisfying life as an independent farmer. But he still has the air of a man out of time. Now that the modern world is beginning to come to Mississippi's hill country, he is increasingly ill at ease, a man no longer at one with his surroundings. He has travelled beyond Mississippi, to New York, Chicago, Nashville, Alabama, Florida, and, the week before we talked to him, Washington. He doesn't much like flying, though, especially over the sea: 'I don't wanna go to Europe. You get up there, you can't see the ground, you can only see clouds.'

■

Napolian Strickland had seemed exhausted when we met him at his house in Como. The strength he had to summon up to do even simple, everyday things made him seem much older than he was. In fact he is at least ten years younger than Othar and Napolian refers to him with a protégé's respect, calling him 'Mr Othar'. Napolian's first cane was made for him by Othar but he learned from his stepfather: 'My daddy, my stepfather, he was a fife blower and a drum player. He taught me to play.' But, according to Napolian, mastering the instrument required more than just knowing the notes, the finger positions, and the timings. To catch the spirit of the music, you had to wait until someone died and then creep into the

Othar's
favourite pigs.

Napolian
breathing life
into the
merrymaking.

graveyard and sit on their grave. Napolian went with Nathaniel Townes, who was a local blues player. Polie sat on the dead man's grave and soon his 'head was getting a little light. I didn't feel right.' He looked over his shoulder and saw a little old black man sitting on the top of the gravestone. 'I run from there, I run so fast.' Napolian refused to elucidate any further; he wouldn't tell us who he thought the man was but he claimed 'that's how I learned to play'.

He learned to play the guitar in a more earthly and time-honoured way – on the diddley-bow like so many other Mississippi bluesmen. 'I started playing with a one-string and a snuff bottle. I played it with a knife. My daddy had a guitar and somebody stole his so I went and got me one.' Yet when he picked up his battered, taped-up Black Horse acoustic to play us a tune or two, old Polie failed to breathe any new life into them. He could not summon up any blues spirits from the past. Sympathy is what I felt as he played *Baby, Please Don't Go.* He performed with an old man's ennui. It seemed to me almost as though Napolian (and Othar, though not so obviously) hangs on to his music as the last reminders he has of an older, more familiar world. It is all he knows in an increasingly complex, fast-changing world in which his music and lifestyle have less and less place.

Jessie Mae Hemphill is the youngest of the three stars of contemporary fife and drum music. She comes from a family whose music has been heard in the Delta for generations. Her grandfather, Sid, was born in 1876 and led various bands throughout his adult life. His bands were recorded by Alan Lomax in 1942, on the same trip that brought about the first Muddy Waters recordings. Her father was a piano player of local repute and her mother's sister, Rosa Lee Hill, was a gospel and blues singer who was recorded on several country blues compilations. Jessie Mae says that music goes back five generations in her family 'to my granddaddy, and to his daddy and to his daddy'. She grew up playing in her grandfather's fife and drum band, playing the drums long before she learned to play guitar.

Jessie Mae made her name as a recording artist singing blues songs and playing guitar but she was brought up in the fife and drum tradition and became an expert drummer. She is still full of sassy self-confidence and to this day thinks she is the best drummer: 'His [Othar's] daughter, Bernice, she calls herself a drummer. She says she beats the drums, but she can't play no drums. She gotta beat real slow, Boom, Boom, Boom. I can't play no drums that slow. And Napolian just love to blow the fife with me. I goed to picnics where he at, he would say, "Let Jessie Mae play, let her play one piece y'all." They wouldn't want me to play. So I would beg 'em and beg 'em until they let me play and that boy would blow that fife and say, "Jessie Mae, I just can't blow until you play the drums. When you play the drums I can really get down." I say, "I see you." He blowed it better for me than in the band he was in.'

The picnic tradition and the fife and drum music that accompanies it were products of, and were kept alive by, the communities in which they existed. When Mississippi's farming was labour-intensive both in the Delta and in the hills around it, the audience for the music was there. Mechanization and the decline of the cotton industry have decimated the rural population of Mississippi, denying the picnics the audiences that were essential for their survival. Thus today's picnics are tame and infrequent affairs. Fife and drum music has suffered more than any other strand of blues because it relies on the farming lifestyle that was its progenitor.

Fife and drum music has been only sporadically recorded. Alan Lomax's field recordings from 1942 were released on Testament Records and others have been parts of the Living Country Blues series on L & R Records. Occasional selections pop up here and there on compilation albums, usually Japanese or continental imports. This lack of recordings is significant: like pre-recorded blues must have been, fife and drum music is improvised head music. It is participatory and communal, changing with each performance depending on audience reaction and the performers' mood. Once recorded, this participation and audience contribution to the

Dancing to the
call of the
drums at a
picnic in the
hills.

process of performance is denied. The recorded version is final and fixed, finishing the improvisation process.

The decline of the fife and drum tradition was inevitable because it was an anachronism as soon as it developed. The African elements that it encompassed and that had been suppressed by the Black Codes (these underpinned slavery and, amongst other things, banned African drumming) were already being transformed by the nascent pre-blues and pre-jazz sounds of the South. Thus the music that the fife and drum bands played was celebrating and re-creating its African roots even as these roots were themselves being co-opted into new *American*-African musical forms. Othar Turner remembers fife players as being a rarity even when he began to play the fife.

As the rural population of the old slave states declined with the mechanization of agriculture, the advance of the boll weevil, and the opening of industrial jobs in the North, the roles that fife and drum music and country picnics played in rural society were being taken on by blues music played in juke-joints and clubs. The baton was passed and the African traditions of audience/musician interaction and musical commentary on community and personal affairs were passed to blues with it. The blues music of Mississippi is flourishing even if the basis of it all, the fife and drum music, is not.

Napolian has now left the house he shared with his mother and the last news I heard of him was that he was in hospital after a bad car accident. Jessie Mae is confined to her trailer-home, half-crippled by illness but Othar is still farming, playing, surviving, and saving old tools for future use.

9

STILL THE DELTA QUEEN

JESSIE MAE, LAST OF THE HEMPHILLS

'I said, you can talk about me, you can say what you please,
Nothing that you say sure gonna worry me.'

I STOOD AT THE TOP of the wobbly, home-made steps that lead up to Jessie Mae Hemphill's trailer. 'The Delta Queen' should have a palace, not a caravan hidden at the back of an out-of-town trailer park. I craned my neck around the huge purple bush I held. It was supposed to be a pot plant, our gift to Jessie Mae, who, I knew, loved growing things in her garden. Peering through the screen door I could see a small, slight woman wearing a pale dress. She was holding a big, old, long-barrelled pistol, thrusting it before as she approached the door. She was expecting us but we were late and, anyway, as she told us later, she never ventures out without a gun.

'The She-Wolf', 'The Delta Queen': not least through her nicknames, Jessie Mae Hemphill's personality was vividly dramatized in my mind, even before I had met her. Photographs of her reinforced the image, showing a confident, strutting woman in her trademark stetson and cowboy boots. Often she wore leopard-skin trousers and jacket or something sparkly and glittering: a two-piece suit, topped with a matching hat. In pictures, she usually held a guitar or leant on a guitar case festooned with labels and blues festival bumper stickers. She sang her own blues songs with an unashamed sensuality that was rather endearing. A female Delta blues musician is unusual enough, and, as one who dressed like an extra in *The Dukes of Hazard*, Jessie Mae Hemphill was quite simply unique; earthy and instinctive with an intelligence sharpened by life, not college.

But the little old lady who opened the door to me looked like a different person. I hated myself for the pity that I felt inside when I saw her. That memory of the sassy, confident woman had gone, replaced irreversibly by the feeling one has for an old lady who needs help to cross the road, or for an abandoned puppy.

Jessie Mae was struck down by illness just before Christmas in 1993. The stroke that she suffered has affected her left side so badly that she holds her left hand with her right when she sits down and drags her left leg, using it only for support. She lost a lot of weight and, though her eyes are still bright and her skin still young, she has the gait of a much older woman. Wigless and half-crippled, she looked more like a battered alley-cat than a she-wolf and in the funky hot atmosphere of her crowded trailer it was a shocking image.

The trailer was cluttered, piled high with enough to fill a small apartment. There were two stoves and a large fridge at one end, and the kitchen area was clean and tidy, the dishes from a recent meal washed on the draining board. She threw down some chicken bones for her long-necked dog and wiped the floor when the dog had finished. A TV flickered silently above the bed, showing a surreal 1960s spy film that starred Richard Harris. Jessie Mae's three Handy Awards sat on top of the dresser next to a photo of her grandfather and another of a church minister. Behind the chair to the rear of the room was a photograph of Junior Parker and a record sleeve of one of her albums.

The mobile home was hot and must be intolerable at the height of summer. There is no air-conditioning, just three large fans. Jessie later told us that the walls are wet all the time in summer.

She put the gun on the bed before she sat down on the chair. Instead of leopard-skin finery, she wore a clean but thin dress and short white socks. The peacock pride of her youth little more than a fond memory: 'I was eight years old and when that Sunday come I went to church and, believe me, I had on that little old dress and black patent-leather shoes and hat dangling with all the bows up in my hair, big bow tied in my head. I thought I was something. But I didn't like my shoes to get dusty, though. The moment they carried me to church I'd be back there just wiping those shoes. Every time my shoe get dusty, I'd stop and wipe that dust off. Mama said, "You'd better come on in, you're gonna be late gettin' to church." So I just keep the dust off my shoes till I get to church then I wipe 'em real good and make 'em shine! Little old patent-leather shoes, I never did wear these old high-top shoes that, you know, children used to wear. I always wore low, quarter patent-leather shoes and when I got big I wore kid-skin, alligator-skin and all of that.'

'What about those hats? How did you come to wear those stetsons?'

'Mmm, the stetsons. See, when it rained, I wouldn't want it to fuggle up on my hair. Somebody would be laughing at me with a cheapie hat on, poking up on my head, so I said, "No, no." I go to north Memphis, to that cowboy store and get me some boots. I wear my boots all the time. I get boots and a cowboy hat, and I bought so many hats. He let me have one for

$70, all the rest of 'em were higher. I set it on my head and he said, "That's you, Jessie." I said, "Let me see," 'cos I love my black cowboy hat. I got me a black stetson, and everybody say, "Jessie Mae, you better hold on to your head 'cos somebody will snatch that stetson off there and sell it!"'

She showed us some other photos, of her in some of her favourite clothes: 'That's my picture. I had it taken at the Handy Awards. I had on my dress with all them sequins on – it was full of sequins, I bet it weighed three pounds. Man, that thing heavy. I've got on my cap and everything, it's got sequins on it too. I started them folks to dressing up coming to that – what d'you call it? – Handy Awards. They used to come up there with anything on, wouldn't be dressed up or nothing.

'I started some white women putting on some clothes, you hear me. I'd be the sharpest thing in there, boy. I had some shoes with the beads all on them and sequins and things, different clothes. Mmm, yeah! I was pretty with my dress, the shoes and the hair and the dress. Lord, them white woman were looking. They said, "Jessie you sure look good." One she said, "I sure would like to get me a dress like that." That cost me $500 but I bought it in Chicago, the brown sequinned dress. I didn't want never come out in front of nobody looking taggy like I was drunk or something, head nappy.

'When I was little, Granddaddy would say, "Are you going somewhere, child?" I was sharp as a tack, did my hair in two long big old plaits and had bows on 'em hanging down on each side of my shoulders. I tell you how smart I was. When I was going to school, you know, I wanted my mama to let me wear a different dress every day and she wouldn't let me. She said, "I ain't gonna be washing and ironing no dress that you wear everyday. If you iron, I wash," so I learned to iron my clothes when I was nine years old. Ironed my own little dresses, starching them too, mind. I ironed them so pretty they be standing out and them little girls be looking at me going to school all dressed up with bows sticking out. I never would do without a bow. And those girls would get so sick of me, oooh, having those pretty dresses on every day. I change dresses every day. I come from school and I iron me one and hang it on side of the wall, that would be pretty in the morning. Wash my socks out and hang my socks, white pretty socks. I bathed every day myself.

'Now I wash my socks the best I can, I can't wash 'em that good, but I wash 'em and there don't be dirty stuff on 'em. I got the dirt out of 'em anyhow. I wash my dresses and put on a different dress every day.'

'That's pretty good with one hand.'

'Oh, yeah. When I get up, I wash this one and put that one on, put me the blue dress on and after I wash it out, I can wear it. I just keep on going until I have 'em all washed out. I've got three washed out now. I just don't let 'em get dirty, I wash it out as soon as I pull it off, and I've got these shoes, size ten shoes! Size ten, where I can get 'em on, you know. See,

Jessie Mae
Hemphill, in
happier times,
with one of her
coveted W.C.
Handy Awards.

they're so big I can easy get 'em on, my toe way down there. I wore 'em big so I don't have to be straining, trying to get 'em on and off, so that is when I got me a ten. I don't know when I could ever wear a six now no more.'

■

Jessie Mae is only in her fifties. Her publicity photos from four or five years ago show a vibrant, healthy woman at the height of her powers. You would guess that she was around forty. Now she looks nearer seventy.

She comes from one of Mississippi's most famous musical families. Hemphills have played all kinds of music around the town of Senatobia in Tate County for several generations. Her grandfather, Sid Hemphill, was a star performer who had his own band for most of his life. He was recorded by Alan Lomax in 1942, on the same field trip that yielded the very first recordings of Muddy Waters' music. Sid's band played blues and also fife and drum music. Jessie Mae grew up with her grandfather who was blind from childhood.

'Was it your grandfather who taught you to sing and play guitar?'

'Yeah, I got it from him. I was his eyes from two years old and on up. I take him everywhere. Everywhere he wanted to go, I would take him. When he would be building things, making things, I would go get his nails for him.'

'When did he go blind?'

'When he were 12. He hit the cotton and the cane split and that little cane spear hit him in the eye, right in the side and put his eye out. He was running from the field, he was running in the cotton and he hit it with the cane and that hog bone back there broke the cane and part of the splinters hit him in his eye.'

Sid later lost his sight completely when he got a cataract in his other eye.

'He didn't just play guitar, did he?'

'Uh-uh. He could play anything. Them flutes and blow fifes, anything, he could blow it. He could play drums, he played killer. And he could play piano, organ, and guitar. Me and him sit down and play guitar together. Oh boy! Everything he play, I learned it.'

'Did he teach you the drums as well?'

'Yes, he teach me the drums and the man we played with, called him Will Head, he teach me how to put a double lick in them drums, you know. Let me see . . . I was about twelve. I was nine when I first start playing the drums. When I was twelve, shoot, I was learning licks myself. Couldn't no man beat me beating those drums, those men they get jealous of me. I'd go to the picnics where they were and me and my mama and aunties and all of them could play drums. "Let the Hemphill girls beat the drums," they say. "We don't wanna beat," my mama used to say. "Well, let the baby play." "I'll let my baby beat," mama tell me. They say, "All right." They be thinking I couldn't beat, you know, and then they be looking at me in won-der when I start to tan them drums and the drum band that was there when we got there, they be looking at one another and saying something when I be beating them drums. They didn't know that I could do that, they just thought I was going to go up there and mess up. I played good drums, I never did bust a drum.'

'But how old were you before they let you play?'

'I was about . . . well, I played at the picnics when I was little, about nine. The drum was so big, up like this, you know. I had to stand on Coca-Cola boxes to beat the drum and some man had to hold the big drum up for me. Boy, oh boy. Granddad say, "I'm gonna let my baby beat the drum for you now. I'm tired. I'm gonna take a break" and I would get on that drum and make more money than Granddaddy would. I make a bosom-full of money. My little bosom would be so full of money and my little pocket-book and white people like y'all would be their throwing money – five, ten dollars.'

'Was it your grandfather who taught you to sing and play guitar?'

'I was full of music when I was born. I had to drag everything out and I was trying to play it. Mama tell my granddaddy, "Are you gonna let that child tear up all of your music?" Granddaddy said, "Let her alone, let her tear it up. I'll buy another." That's what he tell my mama and so they never did fuss at me about it, and I just get the guitar by the neck and carry it through the house, twang, twang, twang, and get it on the bed and pick it on the bed.'

Jessie Mae strummed an imaginary guitar as she told us this, as though possessed by its music, revitalized for a few brief seconds by the memory of playing it. It was almost impossible to imagine her straddling the big bass drum at a county picnic, inciting the wild dancing that Alan Lomax describes in *The Land Where The Blues Began*. But she was there in her slinky white dress, beating out an irresistible rhythmic backdrop to the sexy bucking and grinding of the picnic's dancers.

'Mama would be fussing, "That girl gonna be breaking all your strings" and Granddaddy say, "Let her break 'em. I can buy some more." He didn't care what I done and that's when I learned to play so good. See, when you're fussing a child about a thing, you knocks him back. I never would have been playing no guitar if he had a-been fussing me, but they didn't fuss at me, they didn't care if I broke something. I got so I was playing the guitar good when I was eight years old. I'd sit that guitar up there on my lap and play it. Uh-huh!'

Jessie was warming up now and the lip-smacking relish of her description conjures up a picture of an exasperatingly precocious child. It is a poignant picture, though – the contrast between the spirited child and the crippled old lady only too obvious. I glanced up at the TV just in time to see Richard Harris catch a knife that had been thrown at him.

Jessie Mae became Sid's constant companion and was his contact with the visual world for the rest of his life.

'He was a carpenter, wasn't he?'

'Yeah, he made tables and stuff, chairs. I learned how to bottom chairs with shucks. I learned that from my granddaddy. We take an old inner tube and cut it in strips and make a rubber bottom in the chair. I know how to get that hickory bark and wet it and make a bottom of a chair that'll last for ever. I seed a woman with one about three or four years ago and I says, "I knowed my granddaddy bottomed it" and she said, "He sure did" and it was still there. Yeah, Lord have mercy. And he made me a drum, he made me a violin, and he made me a fife, black at the top, at the mouth part, and silver all the way down. That thing blowed good and you could hear it from here to Como.

'There wasn't nothing that my granddaddy didn't learn me: the size of the nails from a one to a two to a three, four, fives and all the sizes of the nails, tens and twelves and all that. I knowed every nail 'cos he tell me. I was his eyes, you know. I'd go and get the nail. He'd say go get me a five, or a four, or a three.

'I would be helping him, too. I would be handing him things and helping him saw the wood. And if it ain't all right, I'd say, "It ain't even, Granddaddy." He could tell any kind of money, he could tell you a five from a ten and a ten from a twenty, just doing it like that in his fingers and he showed me how to do it, and he said, "A twenty is thicker than a ten" and he knowed a penny from a dime too. Chilluns used to come into the store when Granddaddy had a store and give him a penny for a dime, you know, to get 'em candy, and Granddaddy would feel that penny and would say nothing to the children but tell their mamas. When their mamas come, he would show them the penny they gave for that candy and they would wup their tails, boy they would wup 'em good for giving him that.

'And I could cut baloney when I was seven years old in my uncle's store. He was half-white, married to my daddy's sister. He was named Lou Niles. He was whiter than you and he had brown hair. He had a store and when I was seven years old I would go down there and work in his store. I would go down there and cut the baloney for peoples, you know, and I knowed how to make me change and that. And from then on I could count money with my eyes shut. I could count change out of $100 bill just as good as he could. My uncle learned me how to count the money and Granddaddy learned me too and, shoot, when I went to Memphis, I was good at them cash registers. Everybody who would hire me would put me on the cash register.'

Jessie Mae left her rural life in the Mississippi hills and headed for the seductive big-city pleasures of Memphis, musical capital of the black South.

'I was working in clubs and in cafeterias and in grocery stores, checking out groceries. I work at the laundry, at the White Rose Laundry. And folding shirts, ain't nobody beat me at folding them shirts, man. You get paid by the piece, you know, and, boy. I would have my cheque and it was seventy-, eighty-something dollars every week. I be folding them shirts fast as they be pressing them. I learned them how to fold the shirts, they were folding them some other kind of way. I fold them like when you buy 'em in the store, with pins in there. I'd take it and fold it over this side and then over this side and then take the top back and then pin it at the bottom to the top and then it would be laying out like it in the store. And I learned them how to do it.'

'But you were singing then in clubs as well, weren't you?'

'No. I wasn't singing nowhere but in West Memphis. I go over there sometimes and sing with the boys over there.'

'I read in a book that you sang with B.B. King's band?'

'I used to sing with B.B. when he first started on WDIA, him and Bobby Bland, and then when B.B. got ready to go to Houston, Texas. That was the first place he was booked at: Houston, Texas.'

'You must have met Junior Parker 'cos you've got his picture there?'

'Yup, I met Junior when he was a boy. He had not made no record or nothing either. B.B. hadn't made no record and then he made that "Three O'Clock In The Morning" [*Three O'Clock Blues*], then he made "You Upset Me Like A Falling Tree" [*You Upset Me*]. Boy, that was something else. Whoo! Yeah, I knowed Albert King, Little Milton, Memphis Slim. I played with Memphis Slim in Florence, Italy. That was his last show.'

'What about your nicknames, how did you come to be called the "Delta Queen"?'

'I was called the "Delta Queen", and then this lady came out from Memphis, what was her name? Lily Carter, and she was calling herself the "Delta Queen" and something happened to her, somebody told her or something and she stopped calling herself the "Delta Queen".'

'There was only one!'

'Yeah! I was the Delta Queen and there wasn't no way she was gonna take that and make it her name. She was singing gospel and I was singing blues.'

Jessie Mae's singing did not really become a 'career' – a way of making a living and a means of personal advancement instead of just what she did for fun – until she met David Evans, one of the foremost blues academics in the world. With his encouragement and management, her career took off and by the early 1980s she was flourishing on the festival circuit in the US and over in Europe.

'My first overseas booking was West Berlin. That was a long time ago – the Wall was up 'cos they didn't allow the planes over the Wall and when we would go to West Berlin they couldn't cross the Wall or they would be shot down. When they got ready to go to the airport, they had to turn in front and not cross that Wall, make a sharp turn and come in that-a-way to get to the airport.'

'So when was that?'

'That was in '80 or '81 or something. As soon as they heard that little old cassette I had that David sent over there and them folks sent . . . whatever it takes. They sent it 'cos they wanted to hear me, they wanted to hear me play, and I went over there and was happy and glad going over there. Boy! I thought I was going to have me some money like B.B. and them boys. Whoo, Lordy! B.B. got his money but I didn't get me none, though.'

She is still bitter about the experience and made that very apparent. But this is still a delicate matter, of some controversy, and best left aside.

'So you have been to Germany. You went to Europe lots of times?'

'I went to London, England. And what is the name of that place that I love so much? Rome! Oh boy, I walked out two pairs of shoes in Rome. Walking, looking at them churches, there's lots of pretty churches in Rome. And I had all my pictures of that taken, in the church and inside the door and outside the door and everything. I went in that place where they used to kill folks [the Coliseum], you know that place that broke off at the top, it's a round thing, they show it on TV. Where they kill all them people. The ground was still bloody, still red ground where they killed all those peoples, and I made him take me out. I said I've got to go out of here, I can't stand this, but that's what they did.

'Paris, I stayed in Paris, that was my headquarters. Every time I would go to France, I'd stay in Paris. I've been a lot of places, little bitty places I can't 'call 'em all but, them big cities, I can 'call them. You know, I went overseas so many times myself till I saved enough to get this trailer.'

But Jessie Mae's days of blues stardom, of international travel and world-wide success are over. She claims to have forgotten all her old blues songs and even wishes she had stuck with church singing: 'I didn't care if I thought of no song. I didn't try to think of any. First, they was just coming like somebody writing them on the wall. I would be riding and a song would come to me in the car, that one about "Come and ride with me when the moon shine bright", I made that coming from Oxford one night. Everyone was over there, B.B. was over there, and I was coming from Oxford and the moon was shining so pretty. It were full and I love the full moon. When I was courting, I used to say to my boyfriends, "Come and get me on the full moon. Let's go to the water", and we would go and look at the water and the moon and lay out in the grass, and I was laying back there looking at the moon, and I made that song. The song came like that, it just kept coming, say one verse and the other come just like somebody writing it down. I reckon the Devil must be writing them down 'cos I hear church songs the same way now, church songs come to me the same way, just like that.'

'So maybe God sends the church ones and the Devil sent the blues?'

'Yeah, I would be cleaning up or washing or something or mopping the floor, cleaning up the house and I go to humming, humming, and humming church songs, you know, and I recollect them, the verses just come on out, and I wouldn't know what I was going to sing the next time or anything like that. I'd get to finishing that verse, another would be right there.'

'How did you remember them?'

'They is still in my head now. I ain't never wrote them down, it is in my head now every verse of my songs, my church songs. Now my blues I just forgot them, I went and forgot 'em. I can't hardly sing a whole song of blues for you now. I wish I had kept on singing gospel. I sing my church songs every day. I remember every verse of my church songs and sing 'em; wanna be ready when Jesus comes and I got one, *Do you know him?*, now that's my greatest song. Ooh.'

■

Economic hardship and emotional trauma – 'I woke up this morning and my baby was gone' – are usually found somewhere in the mixture that excites the blues imagination, which provides the inspiration to sing the blues. But repeated, heavy doses of both of these are not the recommended medicine for a healthy and long life. Jessie Mae Hemphill has swallowed her fair share over the years and is now living with the harsh legacy. She is old beyond her years and chronically handicapped by the effects of her stroke. She does not have the money to buy what she needs to make her life more comfortable and she does not have any children to look after her. She is no longer 'The She-Wolf' baying at the bright, full moon, but an old lady telling stories about the good old days and worrying about when her nurse or her relatives will next come to visit her.

'The nurse she come every week, she combs my hair and wash my face and things, bath my back good for me. Get me some water in the house. She's good, Debbie.'

'Did Debbie take you outside today?'

'I got out myself. Nobody gonna take me out there, I go out there by myself. I walk out them steps, walk on out to the road, turn around and come back and sit on that table out there, and then I come in the house, I be scared someone's gonna come around and knock my head off. I have my gun out there with me, though.'

'Do you ever shoot it?'

'Yeah. All the time, the shotgun too. I go around the corner on the highway there, and shot straight up in the air. BOOM! BOOM! Both barrels! I shoot with that shotgun and damn good with that pistol too, I had a 9mm. I shoot it too. Shoot it seven shots.'

'Does no one bother if you shoot it?'

'Yeah! 'Cos they better not say nothing.'

'You don't think that would bother anybody? Would you mind shooting it outside?'

'No! I don't wanna frighten that child.'

The child Jessie Mae was referring to was a friend who was travelling with us but had stayed in the van to sleep off the after effects of a busy night.

'I think he needs a little waking up!'

"Dear, dear, dear. It would wake him up! He'd jump up there and be gone with the truck. He'd think somebody shooting at him and he likely be asleep and he be thinking that I'm shooting at y'all and he'd jump up in the air and he be running. I wish I had a porch light, I'd let y'all do it just to see how he would run! 'Cos he would think, "Jessie Mae went and got mad at them and shot 'em. I might be next!"'

She was more animated than ever, laughing a cackling laugh that made her seem ten years younger straight away and stamping her foot on the hollow-sounding floor of the trailer-home.

Logan, who had finished taking photographs and was sitting on the bed, stretched and put down his hands to support himself, accidentally touching the gun. He started and jumped up.

'You're scared of that gun, aren't you, Logan?'

'I was sitting there and I put my hand on that thing and I kinda nudged it and I thought it was that gun! Oh, that would be my luck to shoot Robert in the ass or something.'

'Sure would! It would go right through you. Kerpow! He'd be running scared, they'd be saying, "Jessie Mae be done something to 'em." Y'all come back next time before it gets dark so I can clean my gun out!'

'I'm not coming back here again when it's dark!'

■

Jessie Mae is alone most of the time now. Those of her family who have not died or moved away are too busy at the casinos to visit her very often, she claims. Her nurse comes regularly and other well-wishers stop by to see how she is doing but most of the time she is left alone.

'So are there any more Hemphills to carry on?'

'No, the rest of 'em don't know nothing. I got plenty of cousins in Minnesota but don't none of them know nothing, they don't know "A" from a bullfrog. I'm the only one left, the last one. The onliest child that Granddaddy had that knows how to do those things, play guitar and pianos, was my daddy. He was the best piano player in the world, my daddy could play the piano, oh yeah.'

'Haven't you got any brothers and sisters?'

'No. I've got some half-brothers in Michigan. But not on my mama's side, there was only me. I used to meet the mailman all the time and she told me the mailman gonna bring me a little brother and I used to go and meet the mailman and say, "Mr Mailman, have you brought me a little brother?" I was a little old somebody about two or three years old and he would say, "No, but I've brought you a sack of cookies" 'cos he knowed what my mommy told me and he would bring a sack of cookies to try and pacify me, 'cos I'd be sure enough mad. Boy, I'd be so mad and feel so bad, hurting my heart when he say he didn't bring one. I go back to the house with my little head down, walking with the sack of cookies, shaking my head. Mom, she'd be back there.

'They shouldn't have done children that-a-way, telling them babies come out of storks and all that stuff. They don't tell them they come out of no stork now, they'll tell you where the baby comes from, any little girl can tell you where a baby comes from now, and when my auntie had her first little baby girl I didn't even know anything about that, I told her she had done ate too many beans! I'd feel her stomach and it would be way out there, you know, and I'd say, "Auntie, you done ate too many beans." I was something like eight or nine years old. We stayed out there and just kept rubbing her stomach all the time and saying she done had too much for supper. She said, "Yeah, baby I ate too much." She shouldn't have been lying to me. And I wanted to know how come her stomach had got so big.'

10 *T*HE FISHING MUSICIAN

BIG JACK JOHNSON

'Don't ask me no more about blues!
Let's talk some more about fishing!'

'*I*T WAS HUGE, bigger than the biggest man. Bigger than Albert himself and he were big! All covered in moss and grass and all that green
stuff you get down in a lake. Yeoooow! It howled at me and came out
of the water. I was gone from there. Man, I was scared.'

Big Jack Johnson himself is big – tall and heavily muscled like a
wrestler. He does not have the air of a man who bothers too much or too
often with fear. But here on his porch, in the dim dusk light, sipping his
beer and gutting his fish while he tells his story, he convinces me that what
he saw that day scared him profoundly. His tale has a conviction to it, and
when a man as outwardly rational and common-sensical as Jack tells you
a tale of the fantastic, it has a chilling plausibility. Childhood fears, of mon-
sters in the dark and beasties in the night, come bubbling up from my
deepest memory recesses like the gases from a rotting corpse in the depths
of a fetid pond.

Jack had been fishing near Helena, at a remote lake, a Mississippi river
cut-off. He claims it had been unvisited for 40 years but knows exactly
where it is and promises to take us there. It was October 1992, the evening
when Albert King played at the King Biscuit Blues Festival in Helena, and
Jack remembers being able to hear the sound of Albert's guitar floating
over the water to where he fished at the edge of the lake. It was Albert's
penultimate public performance. He died at Christmas that year. It was a
calm, quiet evening, still warm at that time of the year.

When this dreadful beast, this Bigfoot, howled, Jack turned tail and
ran.

'I went straight to Frank Frost's house. He lives down there, near
Helena, you know.'

Frank, being Frank, was curious enough to try and drag Jack straight back to the lake. He wanted to see the beast for himself, but Jack dissuaded him and made Frank swear that he would never go down there.

'It was huge, bigger than the biggest man.'

I let the image infiltrate my imagination. It no longer felt the appropriate time to ask Jack too many questions about blues or his musical influences but I was beginning to see how a man with his apparent phlegmatism might have the inventiveness to foster a songwriting skill and a guitar sound that have been described as blues versions of Captain Beefheart's psychedelic fancies.

'How is Frank? Have you seen him lately?'

'Oh, you know, he's still Frank. He quit drinking for a while, but I don't know . . .' Jack's voice tailed off, uncharacteristically hesitant. Frank Frost is one of his oldest friends and was one of the formative influences on his musical career. They have played and recorded together for over a quarter of a century, creating two albums in the 1960s which rank up there with the best of the Chess output of that era.

Nowadays they only play together occasionally. Frank still blows a mean harmonica and sings the blues around Helena, usually with Sam Carr, the drummer from the old band, but he is ill and years of good living and liquid refreshment have aged his body prematurely. Frank is paying his drinking dues and his liver has already packed up once – the hospital had given him a colostomy bag to use while it recovered but he had never bothered to return to have the bag removed. Jack had persuaded him to live at his house while the Johnsons had tried to dry him out, to get him off the whisky – a characteristic gesture of generosity from a man ever willing to extend still further his large family. Jack's concern for his old friend is genuine and unaffected but his help seems to have been only briefly effective, and Frank returned to his own house and to his old ways.

■

Jack Johnson is probably the biggest star in contemporary Delta blues. He is not up there in the international spotlight with Robert Cray or Buddy Guy, but of contemporary Delta bluesmen his reputation surpasses any. Back in the days when his day job was driving a truck, delivering oil all over the Delta, he was known as 'The Oil Man' but he's been able to give that up and make his living from his music. Most people just call him 'Big Jack' now. He tours the US constantly, leaving in his pick-up truck and reappearing days later, having criss-crossed half the country. Earwig, the Chicago record company he records for, have booking agents who organize regular visits to Europe and Japan, and Jack has been able to recruit a good road band, but they tour almost constantly and we were fortunate to catch Jack at home in the Delta.

The Clarksdale neighbourhood where the Johnsons live is on the edge of the town, as close to suburbia as Clarksdale gets. It's not quite white-picket-fence surburbia, though: their house boasts a home-made steel fence that should give it a heavily fortified feel like that of the houses in Beverly Hills but the fence was home-made from the cables and ceramic discs sheared from their telegraph poles during the great ice storm of February 1994. That storm was like the great flood of 1927, reminding Delta residents how precarious their existence was in the face of the unleashed might of nature. I imagine that Mississippians were convinced that Mother Nature had finally been tamed with the river permanently held in check by the levee, but then she crept up and hit them with the ice storm. Charley Patton's *High Water Everywhere* is the definitive account of the 1927 flood and Jack's *Ice Storm Blues* is similarly concise, chronicling just how the inhabitants of Clarksdale survived the worst storm for decades, which left them without electricity for weeks. Needless to say, the song became a local jukebox favourite.

We had arranged to meet Jack at about six o'clock but knew that this time was flexible because he was going out fishing that day. One of his sons told us that he had been out on De Soto Lake since early in the morning and if the fish were biting . . . well, he might be back much later than six. We settled onto his back porch, sipped our beer, and passed the time of day with his son.

Jack's truck pulled in at about seven, so I guessed they had been biting. He had a big tub in the back of the truck, which teemed with fish of all shapes and sizes. It was quite a catch and Jack pointed out the different fish – cypress trout, gar, drum, crappie, and others that he just dismissed as 'trash fish'. He showed us how to skin and gut each one while he talked, deftly wielding a short, blunt knife in his big, long hands. He has a shiny, large face with prominent cheekbones that make him look like a well-fed, younger cousin of Muddy Waters. He's neat, though, despite his size, with a trimmed beard, bright gold teeth, and hair that he teases into carefully gelled whorls before he goes on stage. He chewed tobacco constantly but took care to spit into the street away from the house.

Once we had all exorcized our individual sasquatch demons we got to talking about blues. I asked Jack about his influences – who he had listened to in his youth.

'It was country. I wasn't hearing too much of that blues. I listened to Roy Rogers, Gene Autry, and that Red Foley. I used to hear him on the radio on this country radio station. Now he was a singer, he could sing!'

The country influences are obvious in his guitar-playing, his songwriting, and his choice of cover material. On 'The Oil Man' he does a Merle Travis song, *Steel Guitar Rag*, and reworks the old favourite, *Tom Dooley*, as a guitar work-out, while on the 'Deep Blues' album his own song *Big Boy Now* is a hard-driving blues rap in which Jack proudly recounts the origins of his fondness for yodelling:

OPPOSITE:
Big Jack
Johnson.
The blues tradition he has inherited rests securely on his shoulders.
*Scott Ross,
courtesy of M.C.
Records*

> 'I used to try and yodel like those peoples, Johnnie Cash, Roy
>   Acup, Hank Snow, Roy Rogers, and Gene Autry,
> My Momma said, "Boy." I said, "Yes, Momma." "You can't do like
>   them white folks on that radio."
> I said, "Yes I can, Momma. I'm a big boy now and I can do what-
> ever I please."'

The band lays down a rock-steady John Lee Hooker beat behind Jack's yodelling, guitarists Terry Williams and Ricky Earl cranking out the repeating riff with tight precision.

> 'I'm standing at my Daddy's gate and now I can shoot my old
>   man's .38.'

Jack turns his assertion of independence into one of the most vibrant and powerful statements of freedom and adulthood since Muddy Waters greased up his processed hair, strapped on his guitar, and spelt out his credentials on *Mannish Boy*. Big Jack's song has the same self-assurance, pride, and belief in his own individuality and puts the message over every bit as poetically.

Jack is a master of the acoustic and the electric guitar.

The guitar solo is an incredible series of sounds, completely lacking in the preliminaries that usually lead up to the climax of an instrumental solo.

Jack launches straight into a maniacal, distorted, note-squeezing stream that sounds like the stuttering of a machine-gun, not the pop of a .38. It is a screeching, tearing, metallic noise, mechanical claws on sheet metal. 'See, I am a big boy now – look what I can do!' Jack is screaming, through his guitar, to his mother, his father, and the rest of the world.

On some songs it is the guitar-playing, not the lyrics, that reflects the country influences: on *Tom Dooley* it sounds as if Carlos Santana had been born in Nashville and grew up listening to hillbilly country guitar-picking before he discovered West Coast psychedelia.

'Yeah, I like to yodel.'

He pushed his aviator-style tinted glasses back onto his nose with the cleaner back of his bloody, bescaled hand.

'Now this here's a drum fish. He's got these little old pearls right inside his head.'

Jack wrenched at the fish head with his blunt knife, trying to dig out the little bony protuberances on the skull, the pearls. They are physiological remains from a more primitive age when the fish probably needed these strange bony horns. Now they are buried deep inside its head and it took Jack much twisting and digging to force them out. He extended a hand, the pearl sitting on his palm.

'Here. You can have that. Just say you was given it by the Fishing Musician.'

He pulled another fish from the tub. This one was long and slim.

'This here skinny one, this is the gar. Alligator gar, he's like an eel. You gotta pull here to take his skin off.' It was tough and very tight and peeled back in one piece like a sloughed snakeskin.

Mrs Johnson came out of the back door, interrupting our circle of fishing chitchat. She waved 'Hi' to us all and rushed past, to drive her friends to their bingo game, she said, before adding over her shoulder as she headed for her car, 'Maybe I should go back and get *my* pocketbook, just in case!'

Big Jack Johnson was born at Lambert, Mississippi, on 30 July 1940. His father, Ellis Johnson, played the fiddle, banjo, and guitar in a local band that played at country parties, picnics, and sometimes in juke-joints. They played some blues but also country songs and dance numbers. At the age of only 13, Jack was sitting in with them, playing acoustic guitar, although he was still too young to sample all the delights of band membership:

'Them juke-houses – I wasn't allowed in there!' he remembers.

He switched to electric guitar and learned to play slide, and by 1962 was working with Frank Frost and Sam Carr in what became Mississippi's finest blues band, the Jelly Roll Kings, or the Nighthawks as they were known then. Jack was still a novice and blues music was more a hobby than a means to earn a living. It was two years before the Rolling Stones conquered America, before they insisted that Howlin' Wolf be their guest on *Shindig*, which was their first national appearance on US television. Thus, they did much to introduce the music and culture of black America to the white audiences, even though it was already the basis for most American 'rock 'n' roll' music. Back when Jack started out, blues was still a local boy clad in ragged shorts, not the spruced-up strutting world-beater that it was to become.

The Nighthawks went to Memphis to record an album for Sam Phillips in 1962 – Phillips was a man who didn't need five skinny, suburban Englishmen to tell him what good black American music was. Another album on a Louisiana record label, Jewel, was released in 1966, but wider national recognition eluded them until much later. A Chicago record producer, Michael Frank, heard them playing in Clarksdale in 1975 and returned three years later to record an album. 'Rockin' the Juke Joint Down' was released in 1979 and introduced their brand of Delta blues to a much wider audience. It also included Jack's first ever recorded vocal. The word was out and it even reached Europe, most notably the Netherlands, where the band, now billed as the Jelly Roll Kings, toured and were rapturously received. Jack Johnson's own album, 'The Oil Man', came out in 1987 and his reputation was further enhanced by the 1990 release of 'Daddy, When Is Mama Comin' Home?', which highlighted his songwriting ability.

Most contemporary blues stars write at least some of their own material. All of Buddy Guy's recent albums, for example, feature some of his own songs as well as new material by other songwriters and covers of old songs. Robert Cray's albums are full of his own songs (or at least collaborations between him and other writers), most of them chronicling the ups and downs of his love life. Jack Johnson is also a songwriter, not just an interpreter and an instrumentalist. His songwriting is different mainly in its subject-matter – he does write about his own personal life but also about wider concerns. He has written songs about AIDS, the state of the nation, domestic violence, Chinese tourists, fast-food restaurants, and, of course, fishing, fishing, and more fishing! Such breadth is unusual, especially in an artist who is also an instrumental virtuoso.

Jack chronicles what he sees around him exactly as Charley Patton did in the 1920s and 1930s. Patton's world did not stretch much beyond the Mississippi Delta and most of his songs derive from his specifically Delta experience – *Pea-Vine Blues* and *High Water Everywhere* are probably the best-known examples. Big Jack travels all over the world and spends most of his time on the road in the US, so his subject-matter is of wider appeal. *United States Is In A Bad Shape* was inspired by a visit to New York, where he witnessed the plight of the poor and dispossessed in big cities. Others, like *Mr US AIDS* and *I Slapped My Wife In The Face* are obviously not

OPPOSITE:
Sweet Sixteen is reborn as a Jack Johnson blues samba.

Delta-specific in their subject-matter. Jack has an innate confidence in his own creativity, in his songwriting ability, which empowers him to tackle such difficult subjects, to cover territory that other blues songwriters might shy away from.

■

Jack finally finished cleaning and gutting the fish. He cleaned up and came back onto the porch to play for us. He nestled into a small chair and cradled a borrowed acoustic guitar, his bulk shrinking it as he curled his long fingers around the neck. He started to play *Catfish*, a Delta classic and still one of his favourite songs. It was first recorded in the 1940s by Tommy McClennan and Robert Petway and became the basis for Muddy Waters' *Rollin' Stone* and subsequently his *Still a Fool*.

Jack's records hardly ever feature acoustic guitar and it seldom figures in his live performances but his mastery of it is immediately evident. He picked up the strange guitar and played – no preliminaries, no trial runs. The melody was cleanly fingered and the rhythmic riff repeated faultlessly. He closed his eyes and shook his head as the effect of the song built, immersing himself in the familiar pattern of the chords. The unaccompanied acoustic guitar is no instrument for the weak-hearted, even on their own back porch, because every imprecision of finger movement, every hesitation of timing, is ruthlessly highlighted. Jack passed this stiff test with ease. He did *I've Got My Mojo Working* with Muddy's vocal inflections and even a perfect Muddy jowl-shake at the end, and his playing was light and melodic, often almost Spanish in feeling, where it is so slashing and psychedelic on his live electric guitar solos. Next he played B.B. King's *Sweet Sixteen*, which was reborn as a sort of blues samba.

'You don't learn it. It just happens when you keep playing it. You never stop learning, you never master this instrument,' he told us when he'd finished and we had congratulated him on the skill of his playing.

Before we left, he invited us in to eat some fish. The kitchen was the biggest room in the house, freshly painted in glossy green and white, like a summer house in a Hockney painting, the colours gleaming and reflective as though a high bright sun shone on them. On one of the walls was a picture of a man with his arms outstretched and a little homily beneath it: 'The fastest growing thing in the world is a fish between nibbling and getting away.' Hung behind the kitchen stove was a new set of saucepans; their size made me feel like Gulliver in Brobdingnag. The biggest, a car-tyre-sized frying pan, sizzled on the stove. It was full of Jack's catch, the fish cut up, filleted, and breadcrumbed.

Jack's kids joined us and tucked in hungrily, but not before fetching bread and butter, drinks, and paper towels for us, always serving themselves last – politely, not deferentially. We ate our fill of fried fish, and enjoyed it all the more because we knew its special provenance.

It was late when we had finished eating. The younger Johnsons cleaned up the kitchen, and Jack asked us stay a bit longer – that way our food would have time to digest, he said. We watched TV for a while and swapped fishing stories; I had to make mine up, never having caught anything bigger than what can be found in a tin of sardines. It was nearly midnight when we left, and Jack had a final gift for us: bumper stickers with 'I Love The Oil Man, Big Jack Johnson' on them.

I saw Jack play at the 100 Club in London early the following year. It is a good venue for blues – low and sweaty, crowded and dark. Unfortunately he did not have his own band with him – the usual sign that a musician has reached only a certain level of success and that the tour promoter cannot afford to pay for the band as well as the featured artist.

Jack came to the stage like a boxing champion, with a towel draped around his shoulders, and a minder barging his way through the audience. The stage has no entrance of its own and can only be reached from the front. Jack played two sets. The first was steady and unspectacular – he was reaching out for the audience, testing their response, trying to build a rapport. He was still a stranger in a foreign land, exposed and diffident, and lacking assurance without his own band and in unfamiliar surroundings. But the Blues Kings, who backed him, are a skilful and sympathetic band, and Jack warmed to them and to the attentive, ardent audience.

The second set soared and his usual confidence returned. The songs he played were safe choices – he knew that a pick-up band and a strange audience might not fully appreciate some of the country-influenced sounds. The more obvious material was played and sung with an imagination and inventiveness that revitalized it. Like most contemporary blues players, he has been exposed to all kinds of blues (and other music) via the radio. Often this can make blues musicians (especially guitarists) sound almost generic – as though they had all been painted in the same Chicago colours. Jack manages to leap beyond this standardization. His guitar solos always seem to be striving, ascending to a dream world in the heavens where the imagination flies free. The Chicago blues seems prosaic in comparison, content to root around in the earthy soil where it began.

I think that Jack reaches these heights because he has so much to give, so much of himself to delve into. He is more than just a blues musician – he is a devoted husband, a responsible father, a generous host, and a fanatical fisherman, as well as a superlative and professional musician. I still have the pearl from that drum fish and whenever anyone asks about it, I just say that I had the privilege to be given it by the Fishing Musician.

11 I LOVE THE LIFE I LIVE AND I LIVE THE LIFE I LOVE

WILLIE FOSTER

WILLIE FOSTER LIVES at Goodrich Street in Greenville, Mississippi. His address is on his business card along with the handle that he is proud to go under – 'Harmonica Parader with Soul! Legendary of Muddy Waters: Parties, Dances, Weddings, Special Occasions'. There's even a musical note logo on the card.

His house is made of brick. Willie is only the second Delta bluesman I've met who does not live in a wooden house. As we got out of the car, he was sitting in his wheelchair on the front porch, a cane in his left hand and a revolver protruding from his right-hand trouser pocket. The wooden pole of his false leg was visible below the hem of his khaki trousers.

Willie shook hands with us. He had dry, leathery hands and long, bony fingers with two bulbous rings on his index finger and a wedding band. He had a clipped, greying moustache and wore a shirt with easy-access popper buttons. He welcomed us in and followed us through the front door, which led into a clean, well-equipped kitchen with a shiny, polished cooker, and next to it two microwave ovens and a stack of evaporated milk tins. A chest freezer filled one corner and a breakfast bar divided the kitchen from the living area next to it. On this there was a small fish-tank with two tiny catfish in it. A giant stopwatch-style clock hung above and two carved wooden heads were at each end of the bar, black and impassive. All over the living room there were photographs of Willie's children and grandchildren, and of his wife. In the living room two televisions stood side by side in the far corner with a video recorder under one of them.

We sat down at the kitchen table and Willie settled into the role of happy host:

'This is my wife, Chesterene. These gentlemens is from England, Chester. She's my sixth wife. Hey, do y'all wanna cup of coffee? Chester, do you feel like fixing us a cup of coffee?'

He was born in September 1921. He wasn't born in a hospital – no one was in those days, especially if they were poor and black. But neither was he born in a house or even in the wooden shack that served as a home for his mother and father. He was born in the field where his mother was picking cotton: she laid down her sack and gave birth to her son, suffering enough in the process to prevent her from having any other children. By the age of seven, Willie was back in the fields, hoeing and picking cotton for 30 cents a day. He did not go to school for long, only reaching the fourth grade.

'I was born in a cotton field, my mother was picking cotton when I was born, I don't know if you all know about that cotton thing, do you? I was not a slave, but it was not that much different in the time that I come up and in slavery times, because slaves, you know, they put you up somewhere, you had to stay, somewhere like a pasture, just anywhere you know. Them children over there, them too little to work but they all go out there and work and we be hungry, you know, and them people, white people, you know, would buy black people and make 'em slaves. You go over there and work that land, you better go to chopping it just like in Parchman [a Mississippi prison farm]. I never did feel bad about that, it wasn't my fault, it wasn't our fault, because they brought us in as slaves.

'I'm kinda glad that I was born when I were, because I have something to express to my children, I can explain it to them, "Oh Daddy, don't tell them about how you were born on a cotton sack, they gonna believe they're better than you are", and I raised you and I was the same man born on that cotton sack. I love the life I live and live the life I love, and I'm always the same way, and I thank God for it.'

He remembers his childhood clearly: 'What do y'all want to know about me? I know everything about me from three years old up till 74.'

'What can you remember about being three?'

'Rode a horse. I rode a stallion, by myself. Three years old. My daddy had a black stallion. At 24, 25, he had a black stallion and he was riding with it but I remember when I was three years old he put me up there and he say, "Carry him on home". Daddy was a drinker, and he put me up there and he said, "Hold that thing". I remember to hold that thing, and I held that thing, and that horse carried me from the juke-house. Daddy carried me with him to where he was drinking, he carried me to the juke-joint on the horse and then when we got there, he thought, "I'm gonna send this boy home. Damn, I can't carry him home now, put him on that horse and let him go."

'I remember holding that thing, that's the only time I remember riding a horse at that young. I didn't ride a horse again till I was eight years old. But in '26 I remember then 'cos my daddy used to plough and I'd go out there and carry him some water and a bucket. And he used to drink that water. I were five then. Then the high water come in '27, we stayed in a gin and I know we all had to bundle up in that gin together. We all slept on pallets, little things on the floor, that was the time of the high water, that was in '27.'

'Were you scared?'

'No, I never been afraid of . . . I never been too afraid over anything.'

'Your daddy, did he take you to a lot of jukes?'

'He used to take me 'cos we were living in the country. Wherever a empty house was, there was a juke. He drank a lot. You drink and it bring out the evil thoughts in you. If you're evil and I'm sitting up here hating you, and I won't tell you now, but if I get me a few drinks I'll say, "I like me them pretty girls but I don't like you." You know, I thought about that 'cos my daddy was kinda cruel and I used to say – I made a song about that too – I used to say, "He was too mean, mean as he were, he were mean all right."

'He talked a lot about this old fella out there on Holly Ridge. This was an old blues fella that died. Charley Patton. Daddy bought a record of him and I used to dance off of it. I remember Daddy trying to teach me how to dance. I was just about four years old too. Four years old and a little bit, he'd ball the jack and teach me that.'

'So when did you first hear a harmonica?'

'I was seven years old, doing my own thing, you know, just by myself. I didn't have nobody to play with, nothing like that, and nothing to play with until I finally bought me a harmonica, and I'd get up on the house and I'd blow that harmonica, that's the only thing I had to play with, no sisters and brothers. Other kids would be out there shooting marbles and whatnot with one another, and when I could go I would go and play with them but a lot of times I couldn't go, couldn't do it.

'It took me two weeks to buy a harmonica. I was carrying water, I had gone to work, I took to carrying water to people at work, pumping water. They give me a nickel today, and the next two or three days I made a nickel and the next three or four days I make a nickel, and I said I'm gonna save up my money, and then the next week, somebody gave me a nickel so I had saved up 30 cents. Paid a nickel to go to town, 25 cents for the harmonica and I had me a harmonica. I kept that harmonica about a year and a half. It had wore out but I didn't know the difference. Hey, Vick. How are you doing?'

Willie pauses to welcome another visitor. Vick is the drummer in his band, the Rhythm and Blues Upsetters. He's a younger man with a perfectly circular potbelly whose shape exactly matches the pith helmet on his head. He greets Willie fondly, with affectionate respect.

'This is Frank Vick, he's my drummer now. Vick, these two here, they's from England where I started out, first time I went on stage was in London. Them two there are from London. He's from Memphis.'

We say hello and I offer Vick a seat. Willie waves away the offer and tells me to sit down: 'He's not company, he's just like home, he's like my kids.'

'So who taught you how to play the harmonica, Willie?'

'Nobody but myself, it's just self-explanatory. There wasn't no radio back in my time, when I bought a harmonica there wasn't no radio, there was just an inspiration, something that I . . . I like the music. I liked the noise, different things don't do that, you know, 'cos you beat on the wall and you hear the same sound, you know: boom, boom, boom all the time. But a harmonica makes bang, boing, bing, tong, ting, toing – different sounds. I just kept on – when a train come by, when anything come by, I'd try to make that harmonica play that sound. That's what I did and when I heard a train I wanted to learn how to blow it doing it like a train, chuff, chuff, chuff. I blowed that, that's the first thing I really learned.

'And then a guy come by with a guitar. He be coming down the road, you could hear him a mile away, playing the guitar. He be just walking along playing the guitar, singing, "Oh baby". I listened to him and I run down the road to meet him and I followed him all the way back just to get the sound. I decided to make me one and I put me a nail up there and a nail down there and put me a piece of wire on it and ding, ding, ding and slide up down it and it go ding, ding, *ding*, *DING*, dung, dung, dong. And I just kept on with it and my fingers would get sore and I would reach and get my harmonica and I couldn't blow my harmonica and pick that too, so I would let that alone and blow my harmonica a while and then I gets tired of blowing the harmonica and I'd reach back to the guitar and do that. The blues is just an expression of life. I realized what that was when I was about eight years old, something like that, because I was just sat around and worrying, about I ain't got nobody to play with. I was feeling blue because I ain't got nobody to play with. I realized between eight and nine that was the blues, 'cos I worked hard, I was thirsty, didn't have time to get a drink of water.'

At 17, and with barely a cent to his name, Willie left the Delta and trod the traditional migratory route northwards. He ended up in Detroit where he worked for three years in the railroad and automobile industries as a grinder, a riveter, and a painter. During World War II he joined the army and was soon posted to Europe. London was his initial destination and Willie made his first public appearance there:

'You know in London a lot of things were tore up. You heard about it, I know. It was really banged up in London, all over, really. In '43, I was in the services and some big stars come over there to sing. A lot of us had never saw a big star like Joe Louis and Betty Grable and Billy Eckstine, Cab Calloway. A lot of big guys come over, you know, and Joe Louis showed what he could do. It was a huge place, I betcha maybe 20,000 peoples was out there. Joe Louis and them was up there and they go up on the big stage and box up there for about five minutes, and Betty Grable come up and

speak to everybody and throw kisses at everybody, and Billy Eckstine get up there and sang to cheer us up.

'Then they say, "Anybody got any talents, any soldiers got any talents? Come on up here, do anything, sing, dance, anything." Some of the guys sang, and some of them danced, and they say, "You can come on and blow your harmonica", and I said, "Before all these people?" and they said, "Yeah. Everybody else, look at them, they got up." A guy got up and I knowed I could beat him, singing, you know, and some guy was playing guitar, just one man and he had a keyboard player who played along with him, and then I got on up there and I blows my harmonica. I blows my harmonica and I didn't know but two things to play, what I figured they might have known, that was by Lionel Hampton, *Hampton's Boogie*. I used to blow that on harmonica, and then when I done that, they all cheered, and I went on by Joe Louis, you know, walked on by them, and they was all behind them big ropes, they said, "You'se good, keep the good works up." I said, "I didn't think it was nothing" so then they say, "Anybody else, anybody else wanna come up and play?" Betty Grable said, "Get that soldier up here that was blowing the harmonica, I like that." They said, "Come on back, soldier, and blow your harmonica." I got back up there and I said, "I don't know nothing but that *Hampton's Boogie*," so they said, "Do that again!" I did that again and they were cheering me so and when I went by that time and went on back to my seat to sit down, they said, "You're really good." Joe Louis and Billy Eckstine, they said, "Keep the good work going but whatever you do, do it the best you can." Well, I been blowing ever since.'

'Do you know the sounds by ear or do you just know there's a certain way to blow?'

'I do the sound by ear. I can't read music, never read music in my life, but I know what's what, by ear. That's just a gift. Told God to show me what to do and what should I do. My mama used to tell me, "Don't play, you don't need to play the blues." But that's what I like. She said, "Yeah, but you're selling your soul to hell." A lot of people say you're selling yourself to the Devil, turning your life over to the Devil. God's the cause of you breathing, the Devil can't give you no breath, the Devil is you or me, you know. If I'm a evil person, if I hate you, I'm the Devil; you hate me, you's the Devil. That's what I think about it. When you see your enemy, then that's the Devil, you know. I saw it just as plain as day, you know. Christ showed me a lot of things and when I got real down to it, I said, "I'm gonna join the church and I'm gonna quit that" and that music stayed on my mind, and Lord, what am I to do with it? And He showed it to me as plain as day: "I give it to you, I give you that talent, use it, the talent that I give you, use it, and you will live." I have lived three scores and ten and four. I thank God, everything I do. If I go on stage, I explain to the people, "God's the cause of me doing this." I don't put God in if it wasn't for God.

OPPOSITE:
Willie Foster –
Harmonica
Parader with
Soul.

You couldn't sit there, you're using God's breath, you're using the air that God gives you.'

'You knew Muddy Waters from before he went to Chicago, when he lived in the Delta?'

'That's right, I knowed him. I heard him play at country jukes.'

'When did you meet him again?'

'I met Muddy in Chicago. I was living in St Louis and then I went over to see Muddy Waters' band. I went to the Silver Slipper or whatever that club was, something else. I went over on Lake Street to see Muddy and then that's where I played and he invited me and he say, "Any musicians wanna play some?" So my cousin told me to go on up there and blow that harmonica and I blowed a song that didn't have a harmonica in it which was *Still a Fool*. I blowed *Still a Fool* but I be trying to sing like him.'

Willie still does a good imitation of Muddy's characteristic deep, slow baritone. His own voice is higher and clearer and he sings the lines faster.

'I been singing, "Well, there's two, two trains running." But now if I do it, I do, 'Well there's two, two trains running' in my own voice but I tried to sound exactly like him. That's when he told me, "Do your own thing." He talked to me a lot, lots about life, how to live your life. If you're playing before the folk, then try to please the folk. You can't please them everything but you usually hit the spot somewhere.'

'How long were you in Muddy's band for?'

'Six years. I wasn't in his band, I played tours with him 'cos I had a band of my own. I was living in St Louis and he would go to Canada or Detroit or somewhere, you know.'

'You would go and play harp with him?'

'That's right. He said, "Man, I don't want nobody to go but you." I learned a lot . . . Little Walter told me, "Do your best. All you got to learn is timing. Make that harp say what you want it to say. Anything you think you can say, make it say it. If you miss a word, make that harmonica say it for you." I said, "I think I can do that." Every time he said four or five words, he take that harmonica and do it. But he always amplified his harmonica, he always got a different sound from a lot of people. Anybody you hear blowing like him means they got a amplifier. I never wanted that sound. I tried it a little bit and I said, "No, that ain't me, that's the Little Walter sound, that's the sound of Little Walter."'

Willie played with the Muddy Waters touring band for several years and remembers playing in Maine, Detroit, Canada, and even at Carnegie Hall. He was paid $300 for each show, which was a considerable sum at a time when, as Willie told us, gas cost about 25 cents a gallon and cigarettes were only 15 cents.

'Tell us about that song you wrote with Muddy and Willie Dixon.'

'Well, Muddy was going to Canada, and we see him and he say, you know, "Come to Canada with us. Do you wanna come?" So I say, "Yeah, I'll come." When I went round there with my suitcase to the place where they were all getting set to leave, Willie Dixon was there. He came to the door with his face all covered in shaving cream. He say, "What you doing?" I say, "I'm here, I'm ready to go." He say, "You ready, you set to go?" "I'm ready," I say, "I'm ready as anybody can be." And Willie, he looks at Muddy, and Muddy looked at Willie and said, "Are you thinking what I'm thinking? Let's make a song!" "What can we put to it?" they say. They tried a lot of different things and worked out the words:

> "I'm ready, ready as anybody can be
> I'm ready for you and I hope you're ready for me."

We was sitting there, working on that song, and I poured myself some gin and they said, "We'll put that in too: 'I been drinking gin like I never drunk before.' No, that won't work." So Muddy said, "Try this: 'I been drinking gin like never before.' That'll do it, that fits." So that's how they did it, right there. We went to Canada and did the song live and I blew on it. They pay me $150 for that.'

Willie can certainly tell a good story, in the classic blues tradition. He may even be telling tall tales (like so many other bluesmen) because he has been telling his Muddy Waters stories for years now, but before he died, Muddy himself was interviewed by *Living Blues* magazine and denied all knowledge of Willie: 'Willie Foster never played with me . . . I know all the harp players that played with me.'

Little Walter had not played much with the Muddy Waters band since *Juke* was a huge hit in late 1952. He toured with his own band, the Four Aces, but still recorded with Muddy and was around enough to teach Willie a trick that has become his musical signature: the drawn-out, cross-blown extended note solo that Willie sometimes holds for minutes:

'He said he had one thing that he would give me and that was make the harmonica go Lnnnh, Lnnh, Lnnh like that, that's a chorus. He said, "I brought that here and I want to keep it, 'cos if I die before you – although I'm younger than you – if I die before you, then it keeps going with you. Put that in every song." Sometimes I holds it, I have held it for a minute and thirty seconds.'

'I've seen you sit there and hold it till I think you're gonna choke,' commented Frank Vick.

'Let me get one here and show you. Is that my walker [walking frame] over there? I got two or three in there. That's it.' Willie is not only one-legged and wheelchair-bound, he is also blind, but he has little trouble finding his way around the house. He fetched the walker, which had a belt of harmonicas slung around it.

'What type of harmonicas do you play?'

'I like Pros the best. That kind. That's a Special 20 and that's a Lee Oskar. Lee Oskars or Pros.'

He started to play and demonstrated the wavering, holding technique that Little Walter had taught him. It was a mournful sound, but playing it seemed to fill Willie with renewed enthusiasm to play and he wanted to call 'T-Model' Ford, a local guitar player who lives near by and often plays with Willie and the band:

'You were saying about T-Model Ford. We gonna call him. Do you have that number he gave us, Chester?'

'Chesterene went into one of the back rooms to look for the number.

'You went to New Zealand, didn't you, Willie? Tell us about New Zealand.'

'I didn't really get to realize a lot of things until I went to New Zealand. I learned how people can pull together and love one another. Everybody just loves one another. I went there, the first time I went there was in '91. I was out there and something told me that God waited till you got to be 70 years old and he's gonna let you see the world. I always wanted to see the world. New Zealand's very different from here. You might see someone come from California and go over there. He get over there and he don't wanna come back. New Zealand is the best place I've ever been to. It is a place like . . . similar to here, but it's the difference to the United States. It's more lovelier people over there. There is not a whole lotta of crime, people killing up one another, and people going around and carrying guns. I won't go on my porch here unless I've got my gun, but over there the police don't even carry guns, I'm telling you.

'In New Zealand everybody clings together. A person would be coming by here and seeing me – they could be on their way to church or anywhere – see me doing something out there in the yard, maybe putting a roof on my house, and they look up and say, "Do you need any help, Mr Foster?" "Well, yeah, hand me that tool down there." He would hand it up. "Anything else, what are you guys doing?" "I'm going to nail this all the way across now." "Well, let me get up there and help you get started." When he get through, he say, "Have some tea" and he come in and drink tea and maybe eat some potato chips – we call 'em "French fries", they call 'em "chips" over there – and eat them chips and drink some coffee or some tea or something, and he say, "OK, bye, see you later."

'They Maoris there, Maoris they call 'em. The Maoris is black. They look white but they got our mouths, kind of big lips, you know, like me. You can tell they're black by the look of their mouths, but all of 'em, everybody, got beautiful long hair, good hair. Some of them have short hair, but mostly it's long. When I went over there, my hair was pretty long. They admired my hair, you know, the guys. One of them guys had a bushy head of hair and then they cut it off and tried to make it do like mine, I said it can't do like mine!'

'So how did they come to hear your music in New Zealand?'

'One guy came over here, a guy named Midge Marsden. He's a blues player, he had been just about all over the world. He comes to Texas to see Stevie Ray Vaughan. He loves to play, he blows the harmonica. He was a rock 'n' roll fan, then he wanted to know what the blues was. He came here, he said it was the first time he had come to Mississippi. He had always wanted to come to the Delta, where the blues was born. He said, "I wanna go there." He had a good band, and they got in a plane and he went to Texas and met a lady there who had a brother here. And she said, "I want you to hear this band," so they got him a-playing and they got me and my band for the warm-up band for the New Zealander band. We got to play an hour or an hour and a half. They said, "Now we are gonna call the star of our show up, Mr Willie Foster!" and I went up, you know, and blows my harmonica and close it out, blows some of my songs. They watched everything and they were sitting at a table just like we sitting here. They just had on ordinary blue jeans, the girl had on a black dress, something like that, but when we left the stage, you know, they said, "Now we expect the other band to start in about thirty minutes, give them time to set up and do a sound-check and everything and then they be up. OK?" I said, "The band come from I don't know where – out of state, from New Zealand or Japan or somewhere", well, I didn't know who they were.'

When Willie came off the stage, the band introduced themselves. 'I said, "Oh, you're not from here, are you?" He said, "No". You know how they talk, we say they talk funny, they say we talk funny, I guess that's just the way we do it.'

Willie could have a second career as a mimic – his New Zealand accent is as accurate as his Muddy Waters one. This is the story he told us.

'So I said, "Where are you from?" and he said, "New Zealand." Oh, I never had heard of New Zealand, I really never had in my whole life. He said, "I like the way you play." I said, "Thanks." "This is Sid, this is the drummer, this is so and so." Just calling their names, he didn't tell me what they played. I said, "I'm glad to meet you" and kissed the lady on the hand. He said, "I like the way you sing too." I said, "Thank you." "I'd like to carry you back to New Zealand," he said. I thought he was just saying something, you know. I said, "Yeah, I know what you mean. Well, it was nice meeting y'all." He said, "Come here. Would you play with my band?" I looked at him: "What!" "Would you sit in with my band?" I said, "Yeah" 'cos I'll sit in with anybody. I said, "I done got to hear you. Where are playing at?" He said, "Here." I said, "Yeah? You all playing in here? Wait a minute, who is your band?" He said, "This is my band. You all was our warm-up band." I said, "No!" I thought he was kidding then but I said, "I'll sit in your band whenever I hear you playing somewhere. Take one of my cards and whenever I hear tell you're playing somewhere, I'll find out and if I'm not playing, I'll sit in with you. I'll listen to you a while", 'cos I really didn't think they were playing down there. He said, "We are playing here, for real." The girl said, "Yeah, we are", and I said, "OK, I'll sit in with you." So I said, "First I wanna hear y'all play, y'all some." He said, "Oh yeah, we're gonna play, we're gonna play about thirty or forty minutes, and then we'll call you up and you do two or three." I said, "Oh yeah." I was looking for them to get up and go get dressed. They got up and went right up there and started hooking up their things, man, and the girl went to grab an amplifier and the amplifier was bigger than mine. It was about like that –'

Willie stretched his arms out like a fisherman who has caught an implausibly large fish.

'Two great big speakers in it – that thing weighed about a hundred and something pounds and she just picked it up and brought it on over and set it down. She must be Japanese. They strong in Japan, you know. And they be moving them things around, getting their mikes ready and guitars, and she got that big guitar and throwed that thing down and tuned it up and got it all ready, set her amplifiers like she wanted and she just standing there waiting and all the rest of the guys got ready, and they hooked up there and they didn't start nothing till they got everything perfect, then Midge Marsden made a sound-check on his microphone, the drummer got back there and brushed at the drums and he stopped and they all waited. Then he said, "Showtime!" and they struck out, started to play and, man, they started to playing and my guitar player said, "Man, look at the woman playing guitar. Look at the whole damn band, they're beating us playing our own music!" Them guys were playing! They flat were playing!

'I sat up there listening and everybody goddamn started dancing. I was watching them, I was listening to the music. A musician, you know, he only looks for mistakes from another band. He looking for all mistakes. Don't care how good they playing, even if they really good they make one mistake or two mistakes. You notice every mistake they make. I sat there and those men made no mistakes, and then they played something else, and said, "We have Mr Willie Foster in the house, Mr Willie Foster, he's a Delta bluesman, blow the harmonica." A lot of people around here know me and I came up, gave me a big hand, and he said, "We're gonna do two more songs and then we're gonna call him up to play with us." Well, I had relaxed myself then, yeah, I'm ready to play with that band 'cos them guys can play.

'He got up there and he asks me a question: "What do you wanna play?" I say, "Anything, anything y'all want, you wanna sing one?" He said, "Yeah, what do you want me to sing?" I said, "Anything." He said, "What about *Sweet Home Chicago*?" I said, "I'll just blow harmonica on it." It sounded just like the record but I know when the harmonica is supposed to come in at and I blowed. He said, "Let me hear you, Willie!" and I blew down the harmonica and, man, after that he said, "Do you know anything by Jimmy Reed?" I said, "I know him, I don't know everything but I know just about anything. Just tell me the key you gonna be in and I'll get my harmonica." He said, "We're gonna be in E." I just grabbed the harmonica, and they struck up. He said, "Do you wanna play it like the record or play it like we play it?" I said, "Let's play it like the record first, and then we'll play it like you play it." He said, "OK, you give me the time", so I started, you know, dum dum, like that, and the drummer cut it and the bass man got it and, man, I said, "Yeah, these folks are ready. They can play just about anything." Then we played three or four more and then he said," Let's do *Insurance* [*Take Out Some Insurance*] my way", and I said, "Yeah, I wanna hear it your way." And they played it a whole lot faster, it had different types of words than "Take out some insurance". They played the hell out of it, and I blew the harmonica on it but I would always play it behind them, that harmonica was swinging out but I was playing where I could hear them when they get ready for their breaks, I hear it.

'After they took a break, he said, "I wanna talk with you. I wanna carry you to New Zealand. It's a long way." I said, "Well, where is New Zealand?" I thought it was somewhere in Japan, some town. "It's about eighteen hours' ride," he said. I said, "In a car?" He said, "No. In a plane." I said, "Shit, you know there ain't nowhere in the world that far." I just thinking to myself, yeah, I'll probably go. I said, "What kind of money are we talking about here?" "We'll pay you a free ticket, and what kind of money would you want?" I said, "How long would you want me to stay?" He said, "Two or three months." I said, "Oh my God, you want me to live over there." He said, "Two months, three months maybe. You decide." I said, "You talking how much?" He said, "We'll give you $25,000." I thought, "They's gonna work the hell out of me over there!" I said, "Well, I tell you what, we'll talk about it later, when we get through playing. Tomorrow we'll discuss it." He said, "OK" and next day he called me and we discussed it. He said, "I can get about fifty plays in three months, and each night you play and you can get paid then or wait till the end. I got a lawyer down there and I'm working with your lawyer." I said, "OK, we'll work it from there, that sounds pretty good," and so, sure enough, he told me he would call me in two weeks and in two weeks' time he called me to check. I said, "Yeah I'll do it." Every time he called my lawyer from New Zealand, the lawyer would call me and explain it. He wrote up the papers, got me a contract. Said, "Are you ready to go?" "Yeah, I'm gonna take a chance. I'm about seventy years old and I have lived three scores and ten so I'm ready to go," and first time I ever went there, they sent me a around trip ticket, $2,000, and that was not to come out of my pay.'

'So what's it like over there?'

'I went all over New Zealand. New Zealand ain't no bigger than Texas. I don't think it's as large as Texas and everywhere I played with them I made friends, playing with his band. I got to teach them a lotta things about blues, 'cos they playing, they be happy all the time. I said, "The blues is a feeling," and that girl said, "Willie told me that blues is a feeling and I realized what it is." Oh yeah, New Zealand, man. It is more like heaven over there, like the people say heaven is.'

■

On the wall in the back hall of the Fosters' house was a poster of Willie and the Midge Marsden Band. It had a lurid pink background and a posed shot of Willie and the band on it. Under the picture was a caption: 'Pink Butts Insulation. With Pink Butts you'll never be blue! New Zealand's Number One Insulators!' I asked Willie about the poster.

'That was a commercial I did in New Zealand. It was right after I was made King of the R & M.'

'What's R & M?'

'Er . . . I forget . . . wait a minute, it's R & M B – Rhythm and Mississippi Blues and that was out all over New Zealand and everywhere I go I was known. All over New Zealand. When I went back there and carried my own band there, they say: Willie Foster and his all-black band, Mississippi Willie Foster and Rhythm and Blues Upsetters. All black.'

'Is that the same band you've got now?'

'No. I don't have damn one of those guys I had over in New Zealand.'

'What's your band called now?'

'It is the Rhythm and Blues Upsetters still but they are a different band. John Horton got back and he got his lady to sing and, you know, it leads to confusion. Muddy Waters taught me that if you wanna good band, never put a woman in a band. She tell you something to do, you know, that you don't wanna do. "I want to do so-and-so." You'll yield to her because she got on a dress . . .'

'Especially if it's a short dress.'

'Yeah! She'll do it. I'll tell you who really started out with me: Tina Turner. She was waiting tables, wore on her a little short dress; she wanted to sing. I say, "You can sing if you want."' Willie does a high-pitched, little-girl voice: '"Let me sing," she say . . .

'She would jump up there and she'd sing and she'd always throw her leg over. Well, see that run a lot of customers away – if a man got a wife and Tina comes by and you watching her, and your wife say, "I see you watching that woman with that short dress on", she's looking so hard and, if the woman don't say nothing, she watch her and then she watch her man and a man can't be still when she starts wiggling. His wife might say something, like, "Get me another beer" and he don't hear, he so busy watching. 'You can't hear me for watching that woman, you know, I won't come here again."'

'So did Tina Turner sing with you before she sang with Ike?'

'Man, Tina Turner sang with me before anybody. I had a three-piece band, me and one guitar and a drummer, and in St Louis that was all we had and we in a Jimmy Reed style. So we playing at the lounge where she was working at and she got up there and she sang and then we played another place, another time and she said, "Come on, then, are you gonna let me sing?" I said, "Tina, you drive my customers away, my fans away." She said, "Oh, they don't care." She be singing with a long mike cord and she'd go all around and rub guys up on under the chin, oh yeah! The women didn't like that and people just got up and walked out.

'Muddy Waters told me not to put no woman in the band, but I had another woman, I had a woman drummer, and the guys would look at her, and she wore a dress and some places I'd play I'd want that drummer to play and she'd be playing those drums and her dress would come up here, you know, with her pretty legs. Boy, she could whup them drums. She plays like Willie Below in Chicago, you've heard of him?'

I'd heard of Fred Below, who played for Muddy and Little Walter, and thought that Willie probably meant him.

'She was a good drummer. I kept her for a long time, I don't care if she did drive my boys mad, when she get through playing she go and get her a beer, go to the restroom and come back and sit down like a lady should. She was never out there moaning at men and stuff like that. I don't mind a lady coming up if she is a special guest star, if she coming up and goes through about three songs, then get off stage and out of the way. I don't want her to be all up there fooling with the guys playing the guitars, "Darling, I love you." The guy's trying to play the guitar. He's got his mind on something else. He's going to miss something – dum, dum, dum – "Oh oh, what key are we in?" In other words, a woman is just a man's glory, she's gotta titillate him in some other kind of way and I don't like 'em in my band. I don't like a wrong move in my band, I don't like to hit the wrong key. I like a good band who listen to one another, and they can cover up for each other. I want a good band and I wanna keep 'em together and treat 'em right, damn right, and they'll play right. I don't want no jealous guy, he bring his woman and some guy say, "Come on, wanna dance?" And she get to dancing and he watching her dancing, he ain't gonna play right. Anything they wanna do, let 'em do it. When I get ready to go home, I'm going home with my wife. I get paid off, I meet my wife.'

'How long have you been married for?'

'Oh, to this girl . . . we've been together going on eleven years. But we only been married for three, we stayed together but three years ago we married. I got kids older than she is, I'm old enough for her granddaddy, I'm as old as her mother. That's her father in there, did you see that guy when y'all went to back there?'

'Are you taking care of him? He's sick, isn't he?'

'Yup, I gave him the opportunity, he's welcome to stay there as long he desires. As long as he lives. We're getting on real well here, he treats me just like I'm the proprietor, I treats him just like he's my father-in-law and then we don't have no worries. He's a little bit older than I am. He's 78 and I'm 74. Her mother and my son, my oldest kid, they were born in the same year, but her mother passed a few years back.'

'What other harp players do you like, Willie?'

'Really, I like any of 'em. I ain't got no special favourites. I did like James Cotton, but I think he blows too much. I like Frank Frost, 'cos I taught him.'

'Frank's quite ill at the moment. Big Jack told us last night.'

'Oh yeah, I know he was down when he left here and went to Helena, but he's up and down and they say he done quit drinking now, that's what they told me. I like Frank. When Frank was a little boy, I was in St Louis. Some people would ask me, "Is that your kid?" I'd say, "Yes" a couple of times to get him in a couple of joints, he was only 17 years old and then when I started playing with him 'cos he learned how to blow the harmonica, I says, "You just blow" and he would get up there and he didn't know nothing but Jimmy Reed style but I learned him that part and after he learned that part he kept on till he learned some more, you know, and I let him play and me and he played another place and they said, "Is that your brother?" And he said, "Yeah, we brothers" and we went for brothers then for a while. He come down here and then I come down here and he cut for Phillips up there in Memphis, and we still went for brothers but when he got to drinking he say, "No, he ain't my brother, he just somebody else tells everybody he's my brother."'

'Where do you get your ideas for songs from?'

'My life. Muddy Waters said, "Do your life." He does a lot of his life in his songs, and he told me, "Don't try and play like me but do your own thing." Then they say, "That sounds just like you, Dan" or whatever your name is, you know, so I do my own thing. I do another man's song but I don't try to sound like him. I see a lot of guys trying to sound like Jimmy Reed: "You got me running."'

Willie's slow, slurred Jimmy Reed drawl sounded exactly right.

'I used to sing "You got me running, you got me hiding." Do it my way. I knows Jimmy Reed, we were raised up together. Born about as far from one another as from here to that street out there.'

'Where did he grow up? Where was he from?'

'He was from around Leland. They call it Leland district but it's out, way out, in the country. He was born out there on Mr Johnny Collier's Plantation. I think I'm about five years older than he was. He had a brother who was the same age, his name was Tom, but he died. But Jimmy Reed left way before me, they moved up there to Duncan or Shaw or somewhere around that creek, 'cos I went to their house and saw his mother out there but there where he lived and then he left there and went to Chicago. But he was born right out here at Donnolly, about seven miles from Leland, east-north-east of Leland on a plantation out there. All them children were born out there. Out there at Mr Collier's. Mr Collier had that plantation before '20, before I was born.'

'Do you see Sam Carr, Frank Frost's drummer?'

'Sam's a good drummer . . . I used to like Sam's drumming, but Sam's got a one-two beat, you know, he's got that little snap, hup, hup, you know. He's used to playing with three people and I'm ogreish but I like that heavy drive, that drive the Willie Below style. Do you know Willie Below?'

'Freddie Below, who played with Muddy?'

'That's right, Freddie Below. A lot of people called him Billie Below, Bill Below, Willie Below, Freddie Below. They called him a lot of different names, you know, a lot of people called him everything.'

He pointed across the kitchen table at Frank Vick: 'He knows which way I'm going. I've got my back to him and he knows.'

'So he's got the drive that Fred Below had?'

'Yeah. Freddie Below, he's dead. He taught Little Walter a lot of stuff and he would make Little Walter blow that harp, make Little Walter make his changes right, with them drums, that's the way he and I do. Now where's T-Model? You got his number, Chesterene?'

She found T-Model's number and Willie dialled it, finding the right numbers while she read it out to him from the back room.

T-Model's phone had been cut off, so Willie could not get through to him. He only lives up the road, though, so Willie sent a message with a young neighbour. It was dark by the time T-Model arrived. He knocked and came in, moving with languid ease, his grin beguiling and mischievous. We'd got him out of bed to come over, but 'that don't matter. My wife just left me but I think I can find another one real quick!'

Willie introduced us and I stood up to shake hands: 'Hi, how are you?'

'A lot better if I was your age!' he said, grinning that grin.

We moved from the kitchen to the living room, through the Western-saloon-style swing doors. Old and new photographs covered the walls, and every table and shelf. There were pictures of Willie's family and friends and one of Willie that was in an ornate, scrolled frame, like an old silver frame except it was made of clear plastic.

The room was hot, uncomfortably so, and made worse by the sweat-inducing plastic cover on the chair I sat on. I moved to the sofa, which had a velvet cover, not a plastic one – a dark blue concoction with a fine, pale thread woven through it like a silver spider's web. T-Model set up the Peavey amplifier, and fixed up a big fan which blew its cooling air on the amp, not on the musicians. He plugged in his guitar and a microphone for Willie's harp. They played, starting with an extended, rolling version of B.B. King's *Rock Me Baby*. It shuffled along, less choppy than B.B.'s original. T-Model's guitar-playing was sinuous with a fluidity that matched the way he moved. Its simplicity was deceptive, though, because when our friend, Caleb, played along on acoustic guitar, he struggled to keep up.

Willie pushed his wheelchair into the room and placed it next to T-Model. They sat close together, almost touching, and T-Model leant into Willie as they neared the end of the song, tapping lightly, almost imperceptibly, on his knee as they reached the last bars.

Willie's harmonica-playing owes a lot to Little Walter, inevitably, but much of his style predates Walter, harking back to an earlier, more rural style. As he had explained to us, he does not use a heavily amplified sound like Walter did, eschewing the distortion that Walter explored for a cleaner, sparer sound. His country-based style sounds more like an updated version of the first Sonny Boy Williamson. There are some echoes of Sonny Terry and that other Walter, Walter 'Shakey' Horton. Mercifully, it is also a sparer sound than many modern harp players. Willie's criticism of most contemporary players is valid – like he told us, 'they blow too much'.

They played a Muddy Waters song next, and now the harp and guitar swung together, the booming, echoing sound bouncing around the small room. Willie closed his eyes and shook his head and T-Model smiled at him, his fingers still moving slickly over the strings of his guitar. The song reached its middle, instrumental bars and Willie completed a characteristic warbling solo. We cheered and clapped and T-Model smiled at Willie.

'So who taught you to play guitar, T-Model?'

'Who taught me? I just find it in my head. Can't read, can't write, can't spell, I can't spell "you". Can't spell "me".'

'But you can play that guitar, right?'

'Yeah, I ain't scared of nobody.'

Willie interrupted: 'T-Model can play anything you want. He loves that same tuning, but he can play anything. When I'm playing with him, I don't have nothing but an A sharp and a B flat. He sure can play.'

'I had done went to bed when Willie called me,' said T-Model.

Willie interrupted him again, 'I have called him at four o'clock in the morning and said, "Come on over." He'll come any time I tell him. Any time I say to T-Model, "Wanna help me play some?" he say, "Yeah!" I say, "We gonna be there at four o'clock." He be there at 3.30. He always on time. You can't find many people that do that.'

Willie's got a record out now: *I Found Joy* on Palindrome Records from Texas. It's a good record too, even if it sometimes shows off Willie's songwriting and singing (as well as Bobby Mack's guitar-playing) at the expense of his lovely harp skills. It is well recorded and professionally designed and captures the character of both him and his harp-playing. He's even been paid properly – he had received a cheque from Texas in the post the day we visited. 'I used to be sad, now I done found joy' he sings on the title track in his inimitable tight-jawed way. It sounds like he is trying to stop his false teeth falling out but somehow still conveys the happiness of a man who is enjoying his belated but deserved success, despite losing his sight and a leg. He deserves it too, for his hospitality and kindness mark him out as a true gentleman who has retained such qualities in circumstances where many have lost theirs.

When we left him, late at night after he had entertained us all evening, we asked if we might pay him another visit.

'Any time your heart decide,' he replied.

12 *T*HE KING IS DEAD, LONG LIVE THE KING

MEMPHIS BLUES TODAY – LITTLE JIMMY KING AND THE HOLLYWOOD ALL STARS

'There are more good musicians not playing in Memphis than there are playing.'

MUSEUMS REVEAL A LOT about a city. The larger, municipal museums full of dusty glass cabinets containing incomplete or impossibly old prehistoric animals reveal the usual pretensions of large cities. More interesting are the specialist, usually privately run, museums that most smaller cities have. They betray the city's obsessions, the historical baggage that it carries, the chips it still has on its shoulders.

The Blues Museum on Beale Street in Memphis is exactly like this. It is full of mementoes to the history of the city's music – record sleeves, song-sheets, and musical instruments that date back to the days when Beale Street was a thriving centre of music, drinking, gambling, and whoring. The music that this memorabilia chronicles was the city's greatest gift to the world, greater than the supermarkets and drive-in fast-food restaurants that Memphis also lays claim to, but harder to live with and more challenging to nurture.

There are other artefacts from the pre-music era, from the time before blues when the music was a slave's anguished field-holler. The most conspicuous of these are the restraints: leg-irons, shackles, and the like. Only about thirty years before the birth of the blues music that the museum celebrates, and about six or seven generations before the 1990s, these medieval contraptions were used by the good white folk of Memphis and the surrounding states to imprison their slaves. The display culminates in a pair of leg-irons which must have been for particularly ruthless restraining – the hoops that encircle the ankles are slightly larger than usual, not to make them more comfortable but to accommodate a vicious circle of sharp spikes *inside* the fetters.

There is also a cabinet with a display of bills of sale, complete with descriptions of the slaves for sale. The nearest comparisons are the newspapers' classified advertisements for used cars. Instead of 'good runner', 'low mileage', 'only one careful owner', these read 'Very fine worker', 'Slim but hard working', 'A1 worker', 'Prime girl', 'Good plowman', and on another bill, the bargain basement: 'Ruptured', 'Discard', 'Good for housework only'.

'Sticks and stones may break my bones but words will never hurt me' runs the school-yard rhyme but the adage has nothing to say about how hard and how frequently the sticks and stones were thrown and how defenceless their targets were.

Memphis is still engaged in an everyday struggle to deal with the consequences of its segregated past. The Civil Rights Act may have been passed in 1964 but most of the city's neighbourhoods are still 'black' or 'white'; very few are integrated. Although Memphis has had a largely black administration and local government since those civil rights victories in the 1960s, the racism that the segregation system legalized is still there, simmering under the surface. On several visits to the city I have always noticed that there are numerous social events and particular bars and clubs where the racial mix is . . . not mixed. The usual criticisms of local government corruption and foul play that appear in local papers all over the world are just as common in Memphis' local press, but they are usually tainted by a veiled racism. I've been to all-white social occasions where the 'of course, they're corrupt: they're black' criticisms were quite openly expressed. The stories that the Blues Museum told demonstrated that emotions are still the driving force that shape the contradictory and fluctuating character of the city. From both sides of the racial divide these emotions are a confused mixture of guilt, bigotry, and resentment.

Leaving the museum, I took a walk to clear my head of the images of medieval torture that had been so unsettling. Walking is revealing in itself because the only people who are on foot in downtown Memphis are those who are too poor to own a car and that usually means they are black. My walk took me past the Salvation Army hostel, which was as busy as a prison at exercise time and looked like a fortified school with a high steel fence surrounding the paved yard.

Memphis, Tennessee. The very name conjures up images of music and musicians. The city was one of the most important centres for music-making during the period that saw the transformation of American popular music into the world's rock music. Along with New Orleans and Chicago it provided a soundtrack to adolescence for millions around the world. Today it often seems to be living on its reputation and it can be hard to find good music on even a weekend night in the city. You can always hear blues or soul music down on Beale Street but the tourist haunts there can sometimes be too inhibiting and too irritating. More neighbourly and more locally appreciated music is a better option but harder to find.

Having been so haunted by the images of exploitation and expropriation in the Blues Museum, I needed the restorative boost of local blues – the tourist-free, neighbourhood-bar variety. Unfortunately these are just the venues that don't appear in *The Memphis Flyer*, the weekly arts and entertainment listings magazine of the city.

B.B. King's Blues Club, the Rum Boogie Café, and the Blues City Café regularly feature good blues but have names that are calculatedly cashing in on the tourist market, deliberately putting themselves on the tourist trail. They did not fit the bill. Willie Mitchell has a club which I had never been to and a recent passion for Al Green's sexy sanctifying suggested that this would be a good bet. The club is always in *The Flyer* but their listing never gives the name of a band; it just reads 'live music on weekends'. I rang them but their telephonist spotted my foreigner's accent and assumed I was a tourist. She promised a band who could do anything out of *The Blues Brothers* movie! I thought of the Blues Museum images of exploitation again, and of the racist stereotypes engendered by the blacked-up performers of the nineteenth-century minstrel shows – no, a Blues Brothers cover band was not what I needed.

The friends I was to go out with were close to giving up on blues and settling for a movie, but Los Angeles was the place for movies just as Memphis was the place for music. We were getting desperate but there was one option to try. Lucky Carter is a Memphis musician whose number we had from a mutual friend in London. Apparently he played in the city regularly although we had found no sign of him in any of the listings papers. We decided to try calling him and he answered. He told us that he was playing at a neighbourhood club called Wild Bill's, on the corner of Avalon and Valentine. It was not far away and was promisingly off the tourist trail.

■

We arrived at Wild Bill's soon after 10 o'clock and spotted Lucky immediately. His welcome was friendly and he made us feel at home by inviting us to sit at his table. There he introduced his lady, Mary, whose smart outfit was completed by her eye-catching ear-rings – huge bright-yellow plastic hoops. She was drinking an orange-flavoured vodka drink called 'Tvarschki' which looked like weak orange squash. We settled for quarts of beer, lined them up on the table, and chatted to Lucky about Memphis, London, and the music scene, and to Mary about vodka, Lucky, and Wild Bill.

Wild Bill's club was spruce and clean. The walls were painted pink and the black clock on the wall had a 'Salem – Fresh on the Scene' logo on it.

The crowd was sparse but it was still early and it was Friday the 13th! It had filled up a little when Lucky left us to start the first set. He is a tall, well-built man with enough purely physical presence to command attention even before he started playing. He played a Fender Jaguar guitar and he crouched over it, his long back half-turned to the audience while he settled into his guitar-playing and warmed to the crowd.

The keyboard player, Boogie-Woogie Hubbard, is also tall, but much thinner than Lucky and he wore a European-looking straw hat. He played a cheap-looking Kawai keyboard, although I know he can also play mean blues on the piano – he learned from Memphis Slim. He had a withered, unhealthy look about him and a protruding growth on one side of his head that was not there the last time I saw him play. The bass player wore a lime-green leisure shirt, with 'Florida' stencilled in red stitching across the back of it. He was perched on a tall stool, one buttock on and one off. The drummer was the smartest of the band in a crisp, laundered, white shirt, leather waistcoat, and big gold neck chain. He was also the band leader and called out the keys of each song and counted them in.

They started slowly, feeling their way into the groove, building a rapport with their audience and together creating an atmosphere for the music's fervour to be communicated. They're all experienced blues players who know that they cannot impose a mood on the crowd by starting in top gear. Neither would they want to – they will get into top gear soon enough but as any mechanic or, indeed, driver will confirm, it is not the right gear in which to start. Wild Bill's was filling steadily with a crowd which included several different generations. Three young girls, boisterous and loud, came in and occupied a corner table. Looking around them, they seemed perturbed that they had dressed up so finely and applied their make-up so carefully for such a sedate night in a neighbourhood bar.

The band's choice of song was not particularly original. *Sweet Home Chicago* is one of Robert Johnson's most popular songs and, since *The Blues Brothers* film, one of his best known. But, done with this much care and awareness of the lyrical nuances, it still sounded good. Next they played a slow blues that Boogie-Woogie flavoured with a gospel-tinged organ riff. Albert King's *Crosscut Saw* came four songs, about twenty minutes, into the first set and was the first number to get people on their feet dancing. Lucky was warming to his task, bending the strings of his guitar, extending the notes, prolonging the pauses, so that the silences in his spare, sparse solos said as much as the notes themselves. He began to turn and face the crowd and stretched his long torso, standing taller as he gathered confidence and sensed that the crowd were responding. The band played a compelling version of Freddie King's *Toredown*: slower and more fluid than I had ever heard it, the enunciation of the lyrics much clearer than on King's recorded version.

'We're gonna take a short intermission,' Lucky announced after about forty minutes.

'If you wanna intermission, go see a movie!' quipped one of the crowd.

'We're gonna have a movie,' Lucky replied, quick as a flash, 'it's a sex movie called "Play with Boogie's Organ!"'

The second set was spellbinding. I watched, mesmerized by the relentless passage of the bass player's fingers up and down the frets. Again and again the same pattern of movements was repeated, the same chords fingered out. Like an archetypal bass player, the rest of his body hardly moved, just the fingers, their incessant repetition like a racing cyclist whose legs pump up and down so strongly, while the rest of his body is still. The movement was almost mechanical but the rhythm was alive and animated.

Live blues has a very human, very insistent rhythm and familiar pattern of chords and melody. In the best live blues these create their own small world and the outside world ceases to exist for the listener. There is a John Donne poem in which the poet's bedroom becomes his whole world: 'For love, all love of other sights controls, and makes one little room, an everywhere,' and in another poem: 'This bed thy centre is, these walls thy sphere.'

Physical need broke the spell under which the music held me. At the end of the next song I went to the toilet, out the back of the club, and on my way there I almost walked straight into Wild Bill, who was deep in conversation with a young musician. This youngster wore a lot of gold – rings on several fingers, a prominent false tooth and a chunky necklace. He also wore a T-shirt, which was unusual for a bluesman on a night out, and had long, shiny processed hair which was not. I looked more closely at his T-shirt and realized what was printed on it and why he wore it – 'Little Jimmy King, London 1995'. It was the man himself. Little Jimmy King is one of the stars of contemporary blues and Wild Bill was trying to persuade him to play.

I had heard Little Jimmy at a club on Beale Street a couple of years earlier and not really warmed to his flashy, derivative style. He seemed to have too much of Stevie Ray Vaughan's power blues in his playing, too much speed and not enough finesse. Jimmy's hero and mentor was Albert King and he certainly knew how to bludgeon with the raw power of his guitar-playing but he also knew how to cajole and persuade. Jimmy's adopted name had always seemed to confirm his lack of originality, and I had taken this to mean a lack of quality. The name seemed deliberately calculated to appeal to as many of the blues-record-buying public as possible – from the Albert King fans to the Jimi Hendrix fans. As well as having such a contrived stage name (he adopted the name legally in 1988), Little Jimmy had also tried all the party tricks of the guitar virtuoso – playing with his teeth, behind his back, and through his legs – but had put me

OPPOSITE:
Little Jimmy
King – Long live
the King!

off by using them in an artful manner that suggested he was a guitar hero who had decided to become a blues player, not a blues player who had been acclaimed as a guitar hero.

Little Jimmy is Memphis born and bred. He was born Manuel Gales in 1964. His grandfather was a preacher and a guitar player who, according to the family stories, played on his back porch with Howlin' Wolf. His father also plays and so do his three brothers. Jimmy's father showed him his first chord one Christmas when Jimmy was only six. His elder brother, Eugene, carried the teaching on from there. His recent albums have seen Jimmy heading in a more rock-influenced direction but there was enough common musical heritage for him to slot right in with Lucky Carter's band.

He hadn't brought his guitar with him so he borrowed Lucky's. He leapt behind the microphone, shoved each ring more firmly onto his long, slim fingers, flipped over the guitar (like Albert and Jimi, he plays left-handed), lengthened the strap, and launched into a screaming, guitar-heavy version of *Stormy Monday*. All this was done in one swift, blurring movement as if dramatic entrances with unfamiliar guitars were what he did every night. Perhaps they are. A frisson of excitement flickered through the club. Suddenly the crowd was bigger, more closely packed, and they were sitting straighter or standing taller to see the celebrity, the local boy made good.

In the middle of his first solo he dropped his pick but carried on, picking the notes out with his fingers while somebody found him another pick. Lucky Carter was revelling in the atmosphere and felt the mounting excitement as much as the rest of us. Mary had his video camera with her and Lucky started filming. As the solo climaxed he focused the camera's spotlight on Jimmy. The three girls in the far corner stood on their chairs and cheered wildly. Jimmy responded by playing with his teeth and then behind his back but this time the tricks were invited by the audience, not imposed on them. He played fast, displaying the rock influences on his style, and at one point his right hand was moving so rapidly that I really could not focus on it.

On *Let The Good Times Roll*, he played a more laid-back solo, leaning over the guitar and shaking his head, his heavy crucifix swinging from the gold necklace. Of course he climaxed his little cameo with Albert King's signature tune, *I'll Play The Blues For You* and introduced it with: 'I'll play the blues for you . . . with my friend's guitar'. Since Albert's death in 1992 it has really become Jimmy's signature tune too, and he has had plenty of opportunity to refine his version of it.

Little Jimmy's *tour de force* performance persuaded me that he has taken Albert's name respectfully, as a way of paying homage to his idol. He is not hanging on to the dead man's coat-tails to be dragged along for a free ride to musical success, fame, and fortune. As he told *Living Blues* magazine: 'Albert wanted to leave his tradition with someone. To keep his tradition alive. As long as God gives me the breath in my body, I intend to do it, man.'

Little Jimmy's unscheduled appearance at Wild Bill's and the rapport that he created with the crowd there had banished my Blues Museum demons and shown once more how strong the role of blues was as music providing a communal means of expression and enjoyment. For 20 years the Hollywood All Stars have epitomized this type of local music. Their Hollywood is not in Los Angeles but in north Memphis. It is an unprepossessing neighbourhood that is geographically only a few miles from Beale Street but metaphorically much further away. Surviving despite the comings and goings of musical personnel, the All Stars have played in neighbourhood bars and clubs all over the city and have seldom attracted a wider audience. Lucky Carter was playing with the band now and he suggested we should go to see them the following night.

Their leader and guitarist, Ben Wilson, has become the focus of the band's sound and their de facto manager, the organizer of all their gigs for the past few years. He has the swagger of the city and the raw earthiness of the country in his playing and personality to go with it. On my previous visit to Memphis I had seen him lead a version of the band who were always good enough to complement his own skills, able to switch from the express-train shuffle of T-Bone Walker to the freight-train chug of Muddy Waters at the click of a drumstick and the snap of a snare-drum.

The latest incarnation of the Hollywood All Stars were scheduled to play at Green's Lounge. When we got there, though, there were no ranks of cars parked outside, the aged security guard who used to frisk you as you went in was nowhere to be seen, and the Hollywood All Stars were not playing. The club was nearly empty and Rose Green was not around, which seemed to confirm the rumour that she had sold up to someone from out of town – an entrepreneur who did not have a clue, if the empty club was anything to judge by. We stayed for one beer and were told by another disappointed fan that he'd heard the Hollywood All Stars were playing down in south Memphis at the Club Sensation on Elvis Presley Boulevard. That sounded good – the Club Sensation was a name in a fine tradition of club names like Ernest Mitchell's Club Paradise, where all the blues greats had played in the 1940s and 50s. A secular adjective instead of a spiritual one was just a sign of the times – it was still a suitably hyperbolic name for a club. Elvis Presley Boulevard was somewhere 'you really don't wanna go' according to our informant. What he meant, of course, was that it was yet another part of Memphis that was the 'wrong' side of town.

We piled into our van and went anyway. When we found the place, I started to wonder about that warning: the crowd looked too young for a

Saturday-night blues band and, outside, groups of youths were hanging around menacingly, hands deep in pockets.

Inside, a DJ and master of ceremonies was strutting across the dance floor with a radio mike, like a Jamaican dance-hall DJ. He had the sort of V-shaped torso that takes hours of hard gym-work, but he was friendly enough and pointed us to the table where Lucky Carter and Mary were sitting.

When Ben and the band started playing, the atmosphere deteriorated. Not many of the milling crowd seemed to appreciate the All Stars' music and one of them started adjusting the controls of Ben's amplifier in the middle of the third number. The band took an early break and Ben went to the bar to fetch some drinks. When he got back, another kid was messing with his guitar. I'd already seen the pistol that Ben always carried, and, knowing how protective he was of his guitar, I began to fear the worst. I suspected that he was capable of being as mean as any of those provoking him. He shoved the kid away and started to pack up the guitar and his amplifiers.

'I'm going, man. These guys don't wanna hear no blues,' he told us.

The DJ came back and played even more frenetic music. Some of the dancing was outrageously sexual but all of it was tainted with another feeling, one of menace and danger.

Ben came back from his car: 'Watch it, man, they're mean mothers.' Well, if he was leaving . . .

Lucky Carter and Mary were also on their way out. She said, 'They say you're gonna get clipped, boys. You best leave too.'

Clipped? . . . Thrown out? Robbed? Mugged? We left and discovered in our innocence – and ignorance – that in the gun-happy inner cities of the US, 'clipped', which had always meant 'fleeced' or 'mugged', now meant 'shot', 'blown away'.

After the last, abortive trip to see the Hollywood All Stars, we were determined to hear them play once more before we left Memphis. We called Ben and asked them to a play at a big out-of-town party that we were having. The venue was Uncle Henry's, an old casino on Moon Lake, some way to the south of Memphis. Just how far was to become a matter of some conjecture. It's a famous old building, beautifully sited on an old Mississippi river cut-off. Ben consulted the band, who said they would play, and a price was agreed.

The Exxon filling station on the corner of Poplar and Parkway was the appointed meeting place. The All Stars were going to follow us down in their cars because Uncle Henry's is hard to find, and when everyone was there Ben came over to our van. It transpired that there was a problem: he was willing to go but the other guys thought that Moon Lake was too far.

He tried to persuade them – after all, they had already agreed to the gig and he felt responsible as the leader of the band. No, it's too far, was still the response. We asked him to offer them more money. He went over to the other side of the parking lot where they were parked and was deep in conversation for ten minutes. The answer was still no. The bass player was recovering from a recent heart attack and could not go that far out of town and Boogie-Woogie looked in no state to drive that far anyway. Ben gave them some gas money, which they took. Our hopes rose again. They rose in vain because five more minutes passed and then they climbed into their smart van and drove off. They kept the money.

Ben came back over, despondent and livid. 'That's it,' he said, 'that band are finished.' Apparently this incident was not without precedent.

Their other guitarist came over and apologized. He told us that this was always happening and that 'there are more good musicians not playing in this town than there are playing'.

A year earlier the All Stars had been the best blues band in Memphis, attracting packed crowds whenever they played. Now they were disintegrating in a mess of bickering. Perhaps the other band members resented Ben's assumption of leadership, his assertion of star status. Petty jealousies were upsetting the precarious balance of experienced musicians and strong-willed egos that made up the band.

In many cities, a band as good as the Hollywood All Stars would stand head and shoulders above their musical competitors. They would pull together and set aside their differences in order to keep their regular gigs and pursue their careers. But in Memphis there are so many good musicians and such a wealth of musical heritage that blues bands come and go, form, split, and re-form with bewildering frequency. A peculiarly Southern trait, a sort of self-destructive assertion of independence, plays its part. Perhaps it is the same instinct that made that made Jerry Lee Lewis so utterly shameless about marrying his 13-year-old cousin – an instinct that is compatible with creating memorable, soul-stirring music but not necessarily compatible with turning this music into a career.

13 J*UKE-JOINT BLUES IN THE HILLS*

JUNIOR KIMBOROUGH AND R.L. BURNSIDE

'The hills are alive with the sound of music!'

THE PREDOMINANT SOUND in modern live and recorded blues comes from Chicago. It is played by the blues musicians of Chicago itself, by those in other towns and cities all over the United States, and by blues and blues/rock bands in Europe and the rest of the world. It is also the root of much of the guitar and singing styles of modern rock 'n' roll. The music of Buddy Guy, George Thorogood, the Rolling Stones, Dr Feelgood, AC/DC, and even Iron Maiden is anchored in the same forms and rhythms that Muddy Waters and Howlin' Wolf developed when they left the Mississippi Delta and recorded in Chicago in the late 1940s and early 1950s. It is this music that has been exported around the world. The AAB rhyme schemes and chord patterns of traditional Delta blues were updated with the louder, electric backing that Muddy and his contemporaries used. The guitarists of Chicago's West Side completed the modernization process in the 1950s by playing extended and distorted single-string solos around which the lines of blues were sung. The guitar virtuoso became pre-eminent and the music was ready to be adopted and adapted by several generations of young rock 'n' rollers.

Meanwhile, back down South, in the Delta that Muddy Waters and Howlin' Wolf had left, fifty years passed. Fifty cotton-growing seasons came and went, and another generation of slaves' descendants grew old and died. Another generation, a musical one, had been discovered – aged country blues artists whose musical styles predated those that Muddy Waters had taken north. They were sought out by folklorists, were appreciated raptly at festivals, recorded for Northern record labels, grew even older and died.

The other indigenous musicians of the Delta continued to play, uncelebrated and 'undiscovered' (by the folklorists). They supplemented their musical incomes with a bit of this and a bit of that, farming or running clubs or selling groceries, while the experts exalted the aged, rediscovered stars as the last remnants of a tradition that they claimed was as good as dead and buried. The developers, the innovators, the creators of new sounds in blues seemed to be working exclusively in a new, urban milieu (Chicago, Detroit, St Louis, Memphis, etc.) while the revivialists, the re-creators, kept the original blues alive in the rural areas where it had started.

There was and still is, however, another strand of rural Mississippi blues, which is alive and well in the hills around the Delta. It is contemporary and vivid, not re-creating or reviving:

'S'not dying here! I tell you 'cos we got a lot of young guys and white boys that's playing blues.'

So says David 'Junior' Kimborough and he should know because he's a modern country blues player who heads a whole clan of musicians whose singing, guitar-playing, and song-writing could spread the spark of interest in *contemporary* Mississippi blues that has flared up in recent years.

Junior also runs a juke-joint which attracts musicians and blues fans from the surrounding area and from much further afield. His juke lies just outside Chulahoma, a few miles to the west of Holly Springs, in the hills to the north-east of the Mississippi Delta. The building is set back from the main highway, and on Friday nights, Saturdays, and Sundays it is surrounded by parked cars whose owners are drawn like iron filings to a magnet. People come from miles around to hear Junior play the blues and to hear his neighbour, R.L. Burnside, and his family play too. Locals come from the surrounding farms and towns, drawn like their fathers, mothers, grandfathers, and grandmothers were before them, by the prospect of good music, a wild time, and a chance to dance away the oppression of the outside world for a few hours. Students from nearby Oxford and Memphis come when they have heard enough cover bands in city bars. Blues fans come from overseas to indulge their insatiable need to experience an exciting, vibrant blues tradition.

Chulahoma is in an area of rolling, hilly farmland that never had the large plantations and farms that the Delta itself still had. Instead there are many smaller independent farmers working the land and tilling a soil that is far less fertile than the alluvial deposits of the Delta. The people here are independent, tucked away from the main highways of Mississippi and hidden in their hilly enclave. The music of the hill country reflects the geography. It is an eccentric and concentrated brand of Mississippi blues and its idiosyncrasies of rhythm change and chord patterns have survived the circumscribing effect that recording had on much of the Delta's blues.

Junior's juke-joint does not really have a name. His old juke was called The Chewalla Rib Shack but this one does not seem to need a name. 'Junior's' – that's what everybody calls it. The building itself looks similar to hundreds all over Mississippi. It is made of wood and raised off the ground so that you go up a couple of steps onto the porch. In the centre is the front door with a window on either side. Wooden poles divide the central sitting and dancing area and support the high ceiling. The building used to be a church and the vaulted ceiling that resonated with the gospel sounds of the choir now provides the echoing sound-box for Junior's deep blues. Near the door there's a surprisingly new-looking pool table and beyond that a cleared dance area. At the back is a big jukebox. The selection is mainly blues, ranging from Muddy, Wolf, and the Chicago greats to Tyrone Davis, Bobby Rush, and contemporary blues from labels like Malaco and Ichiban.

Behind the jukebox is a huge wood-burning stove where non-dancers huddle when the autumn and winter nights get really cold. It always pumped out heat but I never saw anyone filling it or stoking its fire. Against the left side of the back wall is what passed for a bar: a chest-high, solid wooden counter with three coffin-sized fridges behind it. They are usually full of cold quart-bottles of beer. On the other side, through some rickety, badly hung doors are the rudimentary toilets.

The decoration is minimal. The timber is picked out with only occasional touches of colour. There is no sign hanging outside to show that it is a juke-joint – the cars and the sound of the music are the only indications. Inside, a few pictures, some advertising material from beer companies, and some handwritten warnings adorn the walls but the rest is bare wood, walls, and floor. The notices say things like: 'No Dope' and 'No Settin on Tables' and are all misspelled with the diagonals of the Ns running the wrong way. The pictures are hand-painted and kitschy like advertising hoardings in India and Africa. They feature beautiful, idealized women, garishly coloured sunsets, bright moons, and perfect, sandy beaches.

On the right-hand side of the building there is a low wooden screen that separates the open dance floor from the tiny band area. Red curtains frame the screen like a miniaturized stage set. Behind it are a couple of stools, a battered drum kit, one small Fender amplifier, and a small heater to keep the band warm.

■

I sat and talked with Junior on the porch, shivering in the ever-colder autumn night on home-made wooden benches. He's a burly man with deep-set, serious eyes and a lined forehead that bears witness to a lifetime of experience and hard work. He has a quiet assurance that inspires confidence. He's been running jukes for over 30 years now and seldom has any trouble. His impassive bulky confidence is one of the reasons why.

'I tell you one thing – blues will never die. The reason I say it will never die now is because we got some young blacks playing it and a lot of whites.' Junior's simple, positive attitude about blues and its survival is inspiring amidst all the academic soul-searching that goes on.

His eldest son, David, has learned from his father and is now a record-ing star in his own right. Fat Possum is a local record label that has released two of Junior's albums, as well as others by David Malone (his son), R.L. Burnside, and Cedell Davis. Kinney Malone, another of Junior's sons, plays drums on his father's album and on his brother's.

Junior does all he can to encourage blues talent and will let musicians from near and far sit in with him though few can add much to the churn-ing, intuitive force that is the Junior Kimborough sound:

'Folks from all around come in here and if they can play, they go back in there and they play. If there's a person who wants to do something and they do it, you know what I mean, I like that. If you could play, you could come here and sit in and play.'

He often finds himself entertaining stars from the rock industry who come down from Memphis to 'rediscover their roots' and hang out with him:

'Two members of the Rolling Stones. They came in here.'

Junior
Kimborough at
his juke-joint
near Holly
Springs
*Fat Possum
Records*

'I heard U2 came down here too?'

'Yeah, that's right.'

'So Keith Richards came in here and had a beer with you. Did you know him?'

'No, I didn't. They came in and someone told me who they was. They had a bass player and a lead player. So I said, "Hey guys, I didn't know you. Why don't y'all come around and play a few?"'

'Did they play? Were they any good?'

'They played with me. Yeah. They were real good and he says, "We wants to do some tunes. That's what we've come for, you know." I said, "Well, that's good. You can listen to me and my boys playing." And when we played, they come and played too.'

'Can you remember which ones it was? Can you remember their names?'

'Keith Richards and . . .'

'Was it Ronnie Wood?'

'I believe so. You know there's been a bunch of musicians coming through here but I didn't know them, you know.'

'So how did you like playing with those two guys?'

'They were real good. They wanted to learn some of my music, you know. And right now they got a record of my music.'

Junior was brought up in Marshall County on the northern edge of Mississippi. He was surrounded by music from a young age – it was the main form of entertainment for his family as it was for many others. He learned the guitar from his brothers and sisters and from family friends:

'If there's not another person playing, you just have to learn it yourself. You see, I've been playing since I was eight years old. I started when I was eight and I quit playing for eight years. I was playing gospel for eight years.'

'And your first guitar?'

'It was a Gene Autry guitar, it had his name on it and everything. I was too young to go anywhere to play. My sister learned me how to play.'

'So who were the big stars when you started playing?'

'My brothers, I had three brothers. Some other people like Fred McDowell and Roosevelt and Eli Green. They were the only blues players. My brother wouldn't let me play his guitar. So, my sisters, they would get the guitar and we could play it all day till he come in. So that's how I learned to play.'

'Did you learn from records or musicians?'

'From musicians. I don't read music, I just play it by ear, but I think I'm pretty good at that.'

Today Junior's blues brother is R.L. Burnside. When we met him, R.L. lived next door to the juke-joint in a house much bigger than most you see in Mississippi. It needed to be because he has a big family: eight sons, ranging in age from 42 to 14. No one, not even R.L., ever mentioned how many daughters he might have. Abandoned cars littered R.L.'s yard, low and heavy on their springs and sunk deep in the hard, rutted clay of the back yard. Behind these was a corrugated-iron hut which might once have been used for storage or perhaps as an outside bathroom. Now it had been surrendered to the ever-encroaching kudzu weed. Kids ran about, playing with their dogs and jumping on the cars.

Often R.L.'s sons will sit in with him while he plays. Duwayne plays bass and guitar and his younger brother Gary plays bass. There is also another generation of Burnside bluesmen – Duwayne's nephew Cedric is only 16 (in 1992) but is already an accomplished drummer. The night we saw R.L., he started on his own. His brand of Mississippi country blues is an electrified, overloaded development of Fred McDowell's blues that R.L. grew up listening to. His guitar style is droning and insistent with repeated riffs and few chord changes. The lyrics are similar, often repeating one or two lines again and again. He plays both the rhythm and lead parts of a blues, which gives him a fat sound with a bottom to it that shifts your feet and gets inside your head. The juke was full of dancers: skinny old men with large young women; young men in baseball caps strutting around the pool table, and lanky older men moving with an oddly disjointed, loose-hipped dance where hands and feet, fingers and toes, all jump and twitch in different directions.

Long Haired Doney is R.L.'s signature tune. He does not sing the last words of the line, finishing it instead with a guitar riff, using the repetition of verses and figures to extend the music for as long as the dancers are still dancing:

> Well I'm gone see my long haired . . .
> Well I'm gone see my long haired . . .
> Well I'm gonna tell her about my troubles.

We went back to Holly Springs the next weekend – we hadn't heard Junior the first time around so this time we got there very early to make sure. A small, brand-new car was parked in front of R.L.'s house, looking out of place amongst the wrecks in his yard. R.L. was on his porch, talking to a scrawny, middle-aged woman. She had oddly hunched shoulders as though she was bent over from carrying a very heavy rucksack, and her grey hair was cropped and greased. She was dressed all in black. Photographic equipment lay strewn all around – it was some kind of photo session for R.L.'s new album. She set up her flashes and screens in front of the hut in the yard and then she sent him off to change into a suit, instead of the jeans and cap he was wearing. She was taking a typical 'bluesman in suit with guitar' shot.

The session took about three hours and was fraught with the usual faulty equipment, changing light conditions, 'right a bit, left a bit, that's good, try it like that' delays. By the time they were finishing, Junior was already playing next door and R.L. looked dog-tired.

Gary Burnside and Kinney Malone were playing with Junior but there was still only one amplifier – both guitars were plugged into it. The drums were unmiked. One of the cymbals had a jagged mouthful missing from one edge, a dusty cobweb hung down from the snare-drum, and puffs of dust billowed out of the amp and speaker cabinet when it was switched on.

A single, angular, harsh guitar note opened the song, followed by a clash on the cymbals and a simple roll on the drums. The crowd had been warming up with corn whisky and were ready for the music to start:

'Come on, Junior. Yes, Junior. Do it,' they shouted.

The drums wandered into action and Junior's guitar settled into that insistent, repetitive loop:

R.L. Burnside and some of his extensive family.

All night long, Junior, I heard you calling my name.
Junior, I love you. Junior, I love you. I hope you love me.

The dancers whooped and hollered and their loose-limbed catharsis after another working week began. The rhythm was booming, warming the cold room, the small amplifier pumping out an impossibly huge, echoing sound. Junior sat on a low stool, hunched, concentrating over the guitar, like a stonemason over raw rock, then looked up, smiling, coaxing rhythm out of the chords he played. There were no histrionics in his solos, no rushing up and down the fretboard, and no grimaces of anguish. He smiled gently and hunched over again. The fingers of his left hand tracked across the frets with apparently minimal effort. They quivered rhythmically as he bent the notes, their movement implausibly small compared with the huge throb of the music they made.

Most of the male dancers held big, plastic Pepsi bottles. There was no Pepsi in these, though, just home-made corn whisky, moonshine, 'white lightning'. We all tried some. It had a strange industrial taste, not nearly so unpleasant as anticipated, with the kick lagging a little behind the gulp, so that the warmth only hit the throat when the liquid was already in the stomach. It worked too, and by midnight the juke was rocking but supplies of moonshine were running low. The big fridges were empty of beer too. We were locked in a virtuous circle of music, moonshine, and dancing, each enhancing the other in an ever tightening spiral. The circle needed more whisky so I went out on a cross-county white lightning hunt with one of Junior's noisier customers. We drove off in his Ford pick-up, whose disintegrating steering made it wobble as sloppily as its drunk driver. He was due in New Orleans at six the next morning to start work on a construction site. We drove to another group of houses a couple of miles away and found the moonshine man inside a trailer-home that was propped up on concrete blocks. The Pepsi bottles were filled up, handed over and we weaved our way back. New Orleans was 400 miles away – my driver was not going to make it.

'You know, I ain't tired of that song,' Junior was saying as we went back inside. He had just finished one number and was strumming quietly on his guitar, as he sought inspiration for the next: 'We got to give it a little time before we get it going.'

The dancers called for more: 'Oh, yeah. Yeah, Junior! Play it, Junior. One more, Junior. Come on! One more! Junior Kimborough!'

One night when I was lying down,
I heard mama tell papa,
You know this boy's playing all night long . . .

The drone started once more, the dancers limbered up, the moonshine flowed and our circle was completed again. The song lurched into raucous guitar and clashing cymbals like a heavy rock solo and Junior's guitar roared like a distorting harmonica.

The Junior Kimborough groove has a sound whose power is hard to convey in words. The source of the power is not volume, as it is with most rock music. Junior and his band do not have banks of amps and speakers to play with, and yet when they crank up, the building itself seems to fill and bounce with the sound they create. It is a moody sound, an old tree whose roots are deep and strong but whose branches are still growing, fresh and green with new leaves. It combines the primeval qualities of the early country blues with the power that electricity gave to Muddy Waters and these create a 'body' music that communicates as much by feel as by sound.

Junior's blues, though produced through old and rudimentary equipment, sounds fresh and new. I first heard it much as I imagine the listeners of the first electrically amplified guitar did: amazed at the power, the pure electric loudness of what they heard. It communicated irresistible dance rhythms and strong emotions with a freshness that seemed to circumvent the 50 years of sounds, songs, and techniques that constrain and restrict so much modern blues. Many blues guitarists have tried to match the technical developments in other musical genres (especially in recorded heavy rock and dance music) by playing faster and/or louder – with more amplifiers at higher volumes. Junior Kimborough's response is implicit in his music: he ignores the technical developments and is freed from the restrictions of the past by playing with a refinement of nuance and touch that no amount of amplification, no amount of technology, can match.

A large part of Junior's uniqueness is that he writes so much of his own material, instead of simply covering standards or adapting existing blues riffs and verses.

'Well, yeah, you see I write my own songs, I write my own music. I don't play nothing of nobody else's 'cept my own music. Well, I tell you, I can get into bed at night and a song starts to coming into my mind and I get up and get my guitar and I play it. If I don't get up then, then I'll forget it.'

We were on the porch again, trying to discover a little more about Junior's songs and their inspiration.

There are many contemporary blues songwriters who write better conventional 'songs' than Junior. Their lyrics mean a little more: they relate a specific story or reveal an insight. There is usually a natural progression from one verse to the next and a certain poetry in the actual words. But few can match the unique power of his *musical* compositions. The setting, the songs, and Junior's unusual guitar-playing with its mournful echoes of country music, its screaming, heavy-rock raucousness, and its funky, soul-music bass create an inimitable combination. Charlie Feathers, Sun Records star of the 1950s, called it 'the beginning and end of all music' when he heard Junior over 30 years ago. The concentrated essence that is Junior's blues might still be too strong for many tastes, but if tastes develop, it might become the mainstream, rather than a tributary to the broad flow of conventional, Chicago-based contemporary blues.

It was late in the evening when Junior and I finished speaking. It was cold out on the porch and the deep black darkness of the Mississippi night had closed in all around. Back inside the juke it was bright and light, warm with dancing, corn whisky, and music. The Pepsi bottles were empty again. Cackling laughter and loud voices drowned out the jukebox.

'Sounds like there's a chicken in there!'

'They've all been drinking that moonshine whisky.'

'Doesn't take too many slugs of that white lightnin'.'

Junior settles back and reflects on another evening's entertaining: 'The blues is not wrong . . . you know, every rock 'n' roll song that I've ever heard is from the blues. The blues made it all but they don't get the credit. That's where the music all started from, the blues.'

By the time I got back to the northern Mississippi hill country, the success of Junior's and R.L.'s Fat Possum releases had made it harder to catch them in their native juke-joint setting. Junior was content to play occasionally, and seemed to be slipping into a becoming and well-deserved semi-retirement. David Malone and the younger Burnsides have taken up the slack and play regularly at the Burnside Palace, their new juke-joint up the road from Junior's place. Junior did not have long to enjoy his retirement – he died suddenly in January 1998.

R.L. is busier than ever and seems to spend most of his time touring in the United States and in Europe. He has made another album, this one backed by a punk blues band, the Jon Spencer Blues Explosion, which is either the 'best blues album in years' or 'possibly the worst ever', depending on which reviews you read, and, I think, on how much other R.L. material you have heard. In the summer of 1996 he supported them on an extensive tour.

His recent appearances in Mississippi have been sporadic but the new generations of Kimboroughs and Burnsides at the Palace are ensuring that their brand of blues hypnosis will bewitch its listeners long after the big name recording stars have moved on to their next pet projects.

14 KEEPING THE BLUES ALIVE

THE DELTA BLUES EDUCATION FUND

'I see so many problems in the world and I wanted to turn these kids around. I see they are headed down the road to destruction.'

'Take a guitar out of a student's hand and it will be replaced by a gun.'

THE COMMERCIAL FACE of the blues shows itself regularly down in the Mississippi Delta. You can rub shoulders with thousands of other blues fans at several festivals throughout the baking-hot summer and early autumn months. The King Biscuit Blues Festival takes place in Helena, Arkansas, close to the Mississippi river itself. Its curious name came about because the King Biscuit Flour Company has sponsored a blues show on Helena radio for many years and now organizes the festival. It has the most picturesque urban setting: the logo-strewn stage is at the base of the slope on the landward side of the levee which forms a natural viewing point for hundreds of fans.

At the tenth festival the logos of the Lady Luck Casino were the largest. The stage was spanned by their two banners, one above and one below. Smaller banners publicized the other sponsors: the Memphis Yacht Club, Helena Rotary Club, Roller Citizens Funeral Home and Taco Bell – a curiously non-bluesy mixture. But all this sponsorship does help bring in the biggest names in today's international blues hierarchy: Buddy Guy, Irma Thomas, James Cotton, Joe Louis Walker, and Robert Junior Lockwood were all on the bill.

To hear these you also had to sit through something that I've come to see as the tawdry, commercialized version of the blues that Brody Buster represents. He is billed as 'The Boy Wonder of the Blues', an 11-year-old blues prodigy whom B.B. King called 'the best blues harp player in the world', but then B.B., for all his wonderful talents, can be rather too free

with a superlative. Brody Buster has a competent band, but they are hired hands with a band leader who directs the proceedings and whom Brody appears to follow slavishly. I would venture that McCauley Culkin and Drew Barrymore, Hollywood stars with ambitious parents, are obvious, and valid, comparisons. Brody has even paraded his wares on Jay Leno's chat show and played at that well-known blues venue, Caesar's Palace in Las Vegas! He can perform all sorts of tricks on his harp but, listening to his performance, I had to search in vain for the feeling, the mood swings, the ups and downs of adult human emotion that surely inspire and under-pin the real blues.

There are even Brody Buster groupies – gaggles of barely pubescent teenage girls shoving their scraps of paper under Brody's nose to get his autograph. Most of them have paid $25 for a Brody Buster T-shirt with its 'You're never too young to get the blues' logo.

Behind the stage where Brody Buster bored an ever-diminishing crowd were the other attractions of the festival. Drew and Shelby were tigers, pacing restlessly in their small cage. They live in a home for 'wild' cats up in the backwoods of Arkansas with their keeper and his family. The keeper had a cleft lip, low brow, and cut-off jeans, and was charging kids $10 for five minutes in the cage with the tigers. Not many were parting with their money. There were any number of craft stalls selling pottery 'made from Mississippi clay' and food stalls selling 'genuine Mississippi catfish', the new staple crop of the Delta. At 1.00 p.m. on Saturday you could take part in the second annual Copenhagen-Skoal Outdoors Arm-Wrestling Contest. Prizes were engraved plaques for the first three places in three different weight divisions.

It was possible to find down-home Delta blues at the King Biscuit Festival. Away from the main stage and past the pacing tigers down on Cherry Street there was another, smaller stage: the Lil' Bit o' Blues stage, where Johnnie Billington and his band, the Midnighters, were playing. They had drawn quite a crowd, a more local crowd. Groups of black kids were messing around on the makeshift seats, attentive to the music but teasing and joking with their friends. Two of them wore LA Raiders base-ball caps, and all of them had hi-top basketball trainers and tapping feet. The girls had slicked-down hair and wore baggy NFL jackets. They might all have been brothers and sisters or cousins of the young kids who made up Johnnie Billington's band.

Johnnie Billington is a musician but he is also a teacher and the Midnighters are his pupils. Informally at his house, and formally through the Clarksdale school system, he has taught the blues to dozens of kids over the last ten years. Those pupils who don't pick up music learn other useful skills, messing with engines or fixing lawn-mowers. He now teaches full-time and his programme is established at several schools in and around Clarksdale.

'Mr Johnnie', as his pupils call him, was originally from Crowder, Mississippi. He worked as a farm worker in the Delta for a number of years before leaving for Detroit to study auto mechanics. From there he went to Chicago where he ran a gas station. He had always played guitar, earning extra money here and there, and when he returned to Clarksdale he spent most of his free time with kids, teaching them to fix engines or play the guitar. As he told Memphis' daily paper, *The Commercial Appeal*, when they came to interview him, 'I love to be around kids.' During the ice-storm of 1994, when the schools were closed for weeks, his house was full of kids; sometimes there were more than twenty crowded inside it. John Ruskey, Director of the Delta Blues Museum in Clarksdale, compares him to 'a character out of a Dickens novel, with this bunch of kids always running around him'.

Mississippi is the poorest and most deprived state in the US and the counties around Clarksdale are some of the worst in the state. One statistic measures what are called Severely Distressed Neighborhoods. These are defined by combining statistics for low-birth-weight babies, infant mortality rates, child death rates, teenage unemployment, juvenile violent crime, high school graduation rates, single-parent families, and families on welfare. Using the figures for the 1994–5 school year, the national average was 6.2 per cent – 6.2 per cent children were growing up in Severely Distressed Neighborhoods. Mississippi was, of course, last on the national scale, and Coahoma County, which includes Clarksdale, had 51 per cent of its children growing up in Severely Distressed Neighborhoods. Bolivar County, next to it, had 78 per cent. (Source: Delta Blues Education Fund.)

The top local bands in Clarksdale are the Stone Gas Band and the Wesley Jefferson Band, both being largely made up of musicians who were taught by Johnnie Billington. He had been teaching kids in his own time for over ten years when the Delta Blues Education Fund was set up in 1993. It gives his work a formal status and enables him to reach more children through the local school system. It also means that Johnnie can now be paid for his work. Organized by John Ruskey, and financed by personal donations and by the Folk Arts Program of the National Endowment for the Arts, the Fund is run on a shoestring budget. For the school year 1993–4 the NEA donated just $6,800 to the Fund, matching the level of private donations. At the same time Harvard, one of the oldest and most prestigious educational establishments in the country, was putting $10m into a House of Blues theme restaurant in Cambridge, Massachusetts, presumably because it represented such a good (*economic*) investment.

◼

The Midnighters played an introductory instrumental. The bass player was not much taller than his instrument. The drummer was even shorter and his nodding head was barely visible above his kit. The keyboard player concentrated intently, his eyes fixed to the movements of his fingers over the keys. At the end of the number Johnnie introduced them: Anthony Sherard on bass, Eddy Dabbs on drums, and keyboardist Derrick Williams. Eddy and Derrick were 13, Anthony just 10. The crowd cheered and the young musicians waved at their friends. Johnnie counted them into a slow blues, potentially much harder to carry off than the shuffle they had started with. They managed it with aplomb, with Derrick's keyboard trilling in the background while Johnnie leant over to whisper a word of advice in his ear. The drummer drove it all on, raising the blues to a crescendo as Johnnie himself took a short guitar solo. The bass player nodded his head, shut his eyes and raised his face to the sky. They were drawing a good-sized crowd by now, even in the chill of the cold wind that was blowing the night-time clouds in and fluttering the awning around their stage. They went into a rollicking version of *Down Home Blues*, an overused blues standard maybe, but done with feeling nevertheless.

Half-a-dozen smaller kids with balloons passed by the back of the stage and a tall man in a bear costume led another. They were followed by a white woman with a Royal Stewart tartan rug around her shoulders. She pushed a black baby in a stroller. On stage an even smaller boy, Marvin Sherard, Anthony's nine-year-old brother, was singing but he was undermiked and his voice did not have the volume to carry over the band.

Mr Johnnie maintains a healthy scepticism for outsiders and their potential for assistance. After all, he has spent a long time teaching kids without any outside help and his bottom line is still: 'What is in it for the kids?'

His work is now paid and formally recognized within the school system, but, despite this and the NEA funding, the programme would founder without the time, effort, and enthusiasm that he puts in. We met him on the porch of his house in Clarksdale, and he looked businesslike and ready to go to work, as usual. He wore a smart, dark-blue suit despite the warm sun and informality of our meeting. Our chat was punctuated by his greetings to passing neighbours, to schoolchildren in band uniform, and to mothers in their cars.

He is fiercely protective of his kids and of the programme itself and still puts in far more than he is paid for. His van is old, and when it breaks down, he spends long hours fixing it. He has to spend his own money to buy food for the kids when they go away for the weekend. Indeed, he claims that on several occasions their parents send them away with the band just to save on baby-sitting and food bills: 'Sometimes they just want their kids outta the way.'

He also has to make sure that the kids do not miss any school if the Midnighters go out of town for a gig. When they have been away for the weekend, he parks the van outside his house. They sleep in the van and Johnnie wakes them at six the next morning, in plenty of time for them to have a wash, eat some breakfast, and get to school on time.

For Johnnie, music is not the *raison d'être* of the programme. Some of the pupils are not musically gifted and so they learn some other skill. He has taught many of them to fix engines: 'I like to teach them not only how to play music, but how to work. I teach them discipline. You find kids who want to do something besides stand on the corner.'

The Midnighters are always immaculately turned out: 'These kids have to dress right when we go to play somewhere. Once they are dressed up, it changes a kid. People give them more respect. I have always dressed up, since I was a kid. I noticed when I went to the store that people gave the ones who were dressed well more respect. So, when I was about eight, I bought a suit for $45, which was a lot of money then. I was working on a farm and I paid $5 a week on it until I got it paid off.'

The first formal lessons of the Delta Blues Education Fund's programme took place on Monday, 3 September 1993 at Friars Point and Roundaway Elementary Schools in Coahoma County. The classes were immediately popular, with kids queuing to enrol. Johnnie found some quick learners amongst his new pupils and formed the best musicians into bands. Before long they were competent enough to become unofficial school bands, playing blues instead of the traditional staples of marching music and New Orleans jazz. The following school year two more schools took up the class – Drew High School and Ruleville High School. Johnnie formed the best of his pupils into a band – the Midnighters. They have gone on to play professional gigs at festivals, clubs, and colleges all over the country.

The programme now has five main teaching objectives. Students will learn professional musicianship, performance skills, citizenship, personal conduct, as well as how to play an instrument. The programme brings together two separate and, until now, diverging parts of the community: the children and the blues musicians. The former will learn a skill and gain an understanding of their heritage while the latter will gain financial reward and long-overdue respect and recognition. The blues will be handed on, as it has been for decades, from one musical generation to the next.

I sat in on a class one afternoon at the Delta Blues Museum. The teacher was not Mr Johnnie but Michael James – 'Dr Mike' to his students. There were six or seven students there. Some of them had been to other classes, and he handed them the instruments that they had already started to learn. A new pupil, Kurt, was having his first lesson. His parents had signed his consent form and he handed it over to Mike. Rapt anticipation was written all over his face. Mike handed him a bass guitar, and he pulled himself onto a tall chair, thrilled to have an instrument in his hand at last.

Mr Johnnie and
the band
practise at the
Delta Blues
Museum.
Panny Mayfield

I don't think he would have looked more excited if had just opened his
Christmas present. Dr Mike showed him how to hold the bass and then
asked another, more experienced student to play some simple notes for
Kurt.

Another student was learning guitar. Mike demonstrated the finger
positions for a particular chord sequence. These were areas of concentration and calm surrounded by the confusion and noise of the other less
attentive kids, brothers, sisters, and friends who were not in the class but
had come to play around. Word must have got out that it was a fun place to
be.

Mike went back to Kurt on the bass guitar. He played a couple of notes,
showed Kurt the finger positions and then sat next to him and snapped his
fingers to give Kurt a rhythm to follow. 'You gotta get their feet working,
getta groove going,' Mike told me.

■

Up in Chicago, a similar programme is operating. 'Blues in the Schools' is
run by the Illinois Art Council, who give grants to blues musicians so that

they can become artists in residence at city schools. The best-known teacher is harmonica player Billy Branch. He plays and teaches his students the harmonica – a perfect instrument for the programme because it is cheap and portable. They also study the history of the music and learn about the life and times of famous blues musicians.

Billy has also taken the programme to other states and cities – Charleston and Columbia in South Carolina, Oshkosh, Wisconsin, and Tucson, Arizona. At a summer school in Helena, Arkansas, the pupils did a public performance of an original song after only eight hours of instruction and practice!

In an interview with *Living Blues* magazine, Billy emphasized how successful the teaching had been: 'Everybody's lookin' to education as the solution and . . . I've never had a case where it wasn't successful. Never.' He likens his role to that of 'mother, father, teacher, counsellor, and everything, you know . . . social worker'.

Johnnie Billington struggles to continue the programme in Clarksdale. It is far poorer than Chicago and money is always a problem. Johnnie is still badly paid for all the work he does. His efforts have not gone unrecognized, though: in 1995 he received a coveted Keeping the Blues Alive Award from the Blues Foundation, a blues Oscar – a lifetime achievement award. It is well deserved. Johnnie is helping the children of Clarksdale learn a rewarding skill, and a means to earn a wage. He is doing as much as he can to give them some choices, some way to escape the economic deprivation that many of them were born into.

Help keep the blues alive. Please send a contribution to the Delta Blues Education Fund at 114 Delta Avenue, Clarksdale, MS 38614, USA.

15 *Cappuccino in Clarksdale*
THE REVITALIZATION OF THE DELTA

FAIR'S IS AN INSTITUTION in Clarksdale. Shirley Fair's restaurant serves the kind of nutritious, old-fashioned soul food that would have the politically correct, metropolitan foodies of the world reaching for their steamed broccoli, sun-dried tomatoes and polyunsaturated fats. We ate our first Clarksdale breakfast there, but stuck to eggs, avoiding the artery-clogging helpings of biscuits and gravy, pig's trotters, and fried everything that made up the rest of the menu. I drank the weak, tasteless coffee that is ubiquitous in the Delta and it reminded me, as weak coffee always does, of student days when my palate was still uneducated to the delights of frothy cappuccinos, creamy *cafés au lait*, and black, oily espressos.

Fair's decoration is spartan. The tables and benches are repaired with odd scraps of wood and painted with broad, uneven strokes, and the black plastic that covers the benches is torn. RC Cola signs hang on the walls and the menu is handwritten. The real attractions are the food and the jukebox, whose Little Milton, Bobby Bland, and B.B. King records gave our egg and toast breakfast a satisfying and galvanizing soundtrack. Clarksdale is poor by the standards of most of the United States and it showed in the tatty clothes and dogged, gulping hunger of the old men who were Shirley's other customers that morning. They ate neckbones and beans and drank the same watery coffee that we were having.

Shirley runs her restaurant, owns a nearby florist's, takes tourists on blues tours of the Delta, and still finds time to greet everyone with a smile. It was busy that morning and she was moving briskly around, but not rushing – this was the Delta – giving breakfast orders to her cook and writing out instructions for her assistant in the flower shop.

With the late breakfast orders backed up on the counter and early lunch customers beginning to come in, Shirley was in need of some help. It came in the shape of Elizabeth, I think her name was, a friend of

Shirley's, a white girl who looked like she had walked out of a 1990s remake of *Gone with the Wind* – a real Southern belle with flawless, pale skin, which she had clearly never had to expose to the midday sun, and long, straight hair pulled back from her high forehead. Her back was ramrod straight, stiffened by the same Southern pride that steeled the resolve of the Confederate officers in the Civil War when they left their plantations and colonnaded mansions in the hands of their wives and children. Elizabeth came to Fair's, a soul-food restaurant, a sanctuary of old-fashioned black culture, and immediately offered to help Shirley. She waited at tables, handing out the orders for neckbones and hamburger steaks to the brown-toothed men who might have had fathers or grandfathers who once waited on her forefathers at their graceful plantation mansions.

Clarksdale, a town that used to be the cotton capital of the Delta, is trying to find a role for itself in a world where cotton is no longer king, a role to take it into the next century. Its people are trying to build a viable future for their town, and to respect and nurture the culture that has done so much to shape the town's past. There is the potential to revitalize Clarksdale without emasculating this culture, unlike the developments on Beale Street in Memphis or on Bourbon Street in New Orleans.

Clarksdale sits at the junction of Highways 61 and 49, the main roads of the Delta, where a host of blues spirits flit up and down on their way to Chicago or Memphis. W.C. Handy lived in the city's black quarter at the turn of the century when it was a flourishing babel of gambling, drinking, and music-making and when it earned the nickname 'the New World'. Bessie Smith died there, of course, when the car she was travelling in careered off Highway 61 at one of the few corners on its arrow-straight length. She was injured in the initial accident and then struck again by a passing car as she lay, stricken at the roadside, before being taken to the local black hospital in Clarksdale (the hospital is now the Riverside Hotel). But by then it was too late for the doctor to repair the damage to her shattered body and she died, and was buried in an unmarked grave.

Muddy Waters was brought up on Stovall's Plantation, a few miles outside Clarksdale, and was first recorded there by Alan Lomax in 1941. John Lee Hooker was born and brought up in the town before moving up to Detroit, and Ike Turner was a DJ on the local radio station, WROX, and led the Kings of Rhythm, Clarksdale's finest band, before he too headed off. He went to Memphis and, in 1951, his band recorded *Rocket 88*, which has the distinction of being celebrated as the first rock 'n' roll record. Robert Johnson, Charley Patton and Son House all interspaced their wanderings around the Delta with semi-permanent stays in Clarksdale, and Eddie Boyd and Earl Hooker were born in Coahoma County (Boyd was born on Stovall's Plantation) and lived in Clarksdale. Little Junior Parker was probably born in Clarksdale in 1932 but the date might have been 1927 and the place might have been Arkansas.

Nowadays Coahoma County's countryside probably looks much as did when Johnson had rambling on his mind or even as it did when Patton was hoboing on the Pea-Vine – miles and miles of flat, black-earthed fields of cotton, stretching to a distant horizon. The crops may be different now, with soya bean taking over from cotton, but the view is much the same. It is a big-skied, relentless view and in summer the sun glares down, parching the land and drying the creeks.

Highway 61 itself has changing greatly over the past few years. Today, it still leads down to Clarksdale from Memphis, but it also lures gamblers to the recently developed casino belt of Mississippi. New, permissive, gambling laws were introduced in 1993 and 1994 and they enticed the casino owners of Las Vegas and Atlantic City to the state like stray cats running to a bowl of fish heads. Between 61 and the Mississippi, on the east bank of the river, stand dozens of new casinos, their huge advertising signs lining the highway from the Memphis city limits all the way down to the Helena turn-off: Lady Luck – Best Odds; Sam's Town – $50,000 Pay Out; Circus Circus – More Jackpots, More Often; Fitzgeralds – Certified Loose Slots.

The Wesley Jefferson Band entertain the crowd at the Do Drop Inn
Panny Mayfield

Where once the road was lined with farm machinery stores and plantation buildings now its enticements tempt the poor and desperate with a thousand 'get-rich-quick' promises. There is even a blues-themed casino. It looks like every other casino except that it has a few pictures of Muddy Waters and Robert Johnson on its walls and a room full of slot machines that is called the Delta Blues Lounge.

There has been a settlement at Clarksdale since before the Civil War but it was only with the completion of the New Orleans to Memphis railroad, which went through Clarksdale, that the town really burgeoned. It was incorporated in 1882 and soon became the most important cotton town of the Delta.

Today its importance as a transport hub has diminished and cotton is no longer the predominant industry, but Clarksdale is still a sizeable town with a population of just over 20,000. It has the wide streets, high kerbs, deep storm drains, and neatly manicured grass verges of so many smaller Southern towns. The streets are laid out in the usual grid pattern and the lazy Sunflower river is the only really distinctive physical feature. It winds slowly through the town, edged by grassy banks, one of which has often been the setting for the town's annual blues celebration, the Sunflower Festival. In the 1940s and 50s Issaquenna was the main blues street. Today it looks a forlorn shadow of its former self – Ike Turner's old club, Turner's Lounge, is a closed-down shell and the New Roxy Cinema is boarded up. There's precious little blues at Smitty's Red Top lounge nowadays, but Gates Piano Shop still promises deals on Wurlitzers and at Mr Bees Mini Mart you can get your hair done in Jerri curls for $25.50.

The Delta Blues Museum was founded in 1979 and is sited, downtown, next to the town's Carnegie Public Library. It's only a small museum and ever according to its own publicity has always struggled for funding. It is and always has been a completely independent and non-profit-making organization, surviving but not expanding through its 30 visitors a month and occasional donations. Until the late 1980s it never had the financial security to enlarge its small collection of records and photographs but a succession of high-profile media events has seen it become securely established since then.

A chance encounter in 1987 transformed this low profile. The story of how Billy Gibbons of ZZ Top became involved is rapidly assuming the status of Delta folklore, like Robert Johnson selling his soul at the crossroads or Bessie Smith 'being denied hospital treatment' because she was black. Long-time blues fan Gibbons had been trying to invest some of his millions (acquired, of course, from record sales of ZZ Top's adrenalin-crazed adaptations of blues riffs) on the stock market in New York and had been put in touch with a broker called Stovall.

'What? You mean, the Stovall Stovalls?' said Gibbons, amazed that this most famous of Delta dynasties might have a family member dealing in bonds on Wall Street. Howard Stovall, to whom Gibbons had spoken, was the grandson of Colonel William Howard Stovall, who had owned the plantation when Muddy lived there.

Inspired by this chance encounter, Gibbons came down to Clarksdale to visit the museum. He was instrumental in launching a $1m fundraising campaign in 1988 and he publicized the museum all over the world by putting its name and address on every ZZ Top release since the 1990 'Recycler' album. In 1989, the famous Muddywood guitar was presented to the museum. It is handmade from a cypress wood plank that came from the shack that Muddy Waters lived in on Stovall's Plantation.

The publicity garnered by these media events has raised the museum's profile immeasurably and other donations followed – B.B. King gave one of his 'Lucille' guitars and John Fogerty (ex-Creedence Clearwater Revival) and Bonnie Raitt have also made major contributions. In 1992, $50,000 was contributed by Benson and Hedges, who had sponsored a concert in honour of John Lee Hooker at Madison Square Garden in New York. This contribution was matched by a grant from the National Endowment for the Humanities. More is promised from that source.

In 1993, the museum had 13,015 visitors. They contributed an estimated $1m to the Coahoma County economy in terms of spending at motels, shops, petrol stations, etc. In 1994 there were 14,361 visitors, and all of these visitors have contributed to make Clarksdale one of the very few Delta towns where revenue from sales tax is actually on the increase – a fair indication of the way in which the local economy is heading. By 1995 the museum had over 16,000 visitors and estimated 2,000 or 3,000 more for 1996.

Nowadays the museum features a greatly enhanced photographic section, a big Madame Tussaud-style display of Muddy and the Muddywood guitar, and a superbly comprehensive account of the area's musical history – complete with photographs, old guitars, and other artefacts. The building is small but a lot is packed in. The gift shop is superb, with CDs, tapes, and books that are almost impossible to get in other shops. There is also an engrossing library (but no café selling pastries and . . . cappuccino!).

Their finances are more secure now and the curator, John Ruskey, can even contemplate a move into bigger, more self-contained premises. A new building has been earmarked in the freight depot of the old railroad station but it needs a lot of renovation and the federal grant application is still being 'processed'.

John Ruskey is an eccentric and eclectic man of a type that I have only ever met in the United States. Sometimes they run youth hostels in artistic communities high in the mountains of New Mexico or Colorado. I once met one who organized cycling trips in northern California. Usually they wear hand-me-down clothes and shoes that don't quite match the rest of their outfits. John rides his yellow mountain bike wearing a smart black suit, frilly white shirt, and very worn cowboy boots. He lives in an enormous old warehouse down on the Sunflower river, sharing the space with a library of books, his four cats, a canoe, and enough musical intruments to equip a whole band, which I think is what he does do with them. The warehouse is large enough for him to ride his bicycle around the canoe and the book-shelves and still have room to avoid running over the cats.

John is a man for all seasons, a talented multi-instrumentalist and songwriter, and an adventurer who thinks nothing of canoeing up and down the mighty Mississippi armed only with a paddle and an almost psy-chic knowledge of the currents and whirlpools that make big rivers so treacherous. He also has an almost insatiable desire to devote himself self-lessly to causes through which he will gain very little for himself. He orga-nized the Delta Blues Education Fund and found the means to raise the sponsorship money and grants that have enabled Johnnie Billington, the inspirational leader of the programme, to be paid for his work.

He runs the museum with a relaxed and informal control and in a way, with his friendliness, open mind, and egalitarian liberalism – allied to an ability to make things happen – that represents the way forward for Clarksdale. He is educated widely enough and sufficiently well-read to be aware of Clarksdale's history and the baggage that comes with it and to have become an integral part of the town's community, but is also enough of an outsider not to be constricted or tied down by the weight of this past.

The success and continuing growth of the Delta Blues Museum has been central to Clarksdale's revitalization. It draws tourists and fans and provides a focus for the rapprochement between those on either side of the railroad tracks that traditionally divided the town, between black and white, 'have' and 'have not' – a rapprochement that is implicit in 'white' Clarksdale's acceptance of the importance and vitality of the music and culture that came from the 'wrong' side of those railroad tracks.

The other role of the museum is in keeping the blues tradition alive. It preserves and records the history of blues but, as John Ruskey says, 'We don't want things just behind glass cases locked away in formaldehyde. We're an active museum in community programmes. We have many great musicians who are still living in Clarksdale and the Mississippi Delta and keeping this tradition alive.' The museum's close links with the Delta Blues Education Fund programme reinforce this active role: the programme now has over forty students taught by four different teachers.

Like John Ruskey, Shirley Fair is able to set aside the divisions of the past in order to build a less divided future. Howard Stovall is the same: he left the Delta, went to Yale, and worked on Wall Street but returned to Clarksdale, to his family and his roots. He even plays keyboards in a local blues band, the Stone Gas Band, which is largely made up of ex-pupils of Johnnie Billington's. Thus the people of the Delta are making a future for themselves. A new generation of men and women are overcoming the prejudices and partialities of their upbringings, and looking to forge a community that respects its past but does not allow it to determine its future.

There are unanswered questions, doubts that lurk under the surface – where are the racist reactionaries who, Francis Davis (*History of the Blues*) tells us, bombed Wade Walton's barber shop in 1960? Are they all dead, buried with their obsolete beliefs? Where are the faceless lynchers in their Hallowe'en hoods who hounded the Northern civil rights workers in the 1960s? Alan Lomax's *The Land Where The Blues Began* contains terrifying reports of the all-powerful bigotry of local sheriffs in the 1940s. The film *Mississippi Burning* encapsulates the violence of traditional Southern racism – opinions expressed as violently as that are held very firmly and seldom change within one or even two generations. Nicholas Lemann, in his 1991 book *The Promised Land*, claimed that the white population of Clarksdale saw the town's black population as 'a welfare colony, floating on a tide of welfare payments, sapped of the will to work', so the opinions are still publicly, if anonymously, expressed. Perhaps these reactionaries are relaxing with their mint juleps at their Clarksdale country club (there is a country club in Clarksdale though it seems almost unbearably anachronistic), where they know the only black skins they see will be clad in spotless white jackets and carrying trays of iced drinks.

■

The economic and social problems of Clarksdale and its surrounding counties have not disappeared just because the blues museum has attracted $1m of new money into the area. One day this money will be the basis for a permanent, long-term economic regeneration and provide relief from the social problems. For the moment these problems are still there. The bare statistics even at the time of writing tell some of the story: Mississippi is well known as the most deprived state in the US and the Delta has long been known as 'the South's South'. The counties around Clarksdale are some of the poorest in the state. The per-capita income of the state is $14,088, the lowest of any state in the US by nearly $3,000 (the national average is over $25,000). It has the lowest expenditure per student on secondary education of any state, and the lowest percentage of students taking SATs (Scholastic Aptitude Tests), 4 per cent, where the national average is 43 per cent. (Source: Delta Blues Education Fund.)

Sid Graves, the first Director of the Delta Blues Museum, was horrified by the poverty when he returned to Mississippi from the North. Conditions never seemed to be alleviated by economic booms in other parts of the country: 'Even in the early Reagan years nothing ever trickled down here.' Nowadays the traditional problems of economic hardship are compounded by what have previously been considered purely Northern or big-city problems: gang wars, drugs-related crime, and street muggings have all become commonplace in the larger towns of the Delta, including Clarksdale.

In a way the personal tales of hardship and poverty paint a more vivid picture than the statistics: the crack-addict mother feeding her one-year-old baby to a pool full of snapper turtles because she did not have enough money to feed her habit and her baby; the drive-by shooting that we saw at a motel just inside the Clarksdale city limits on Highway 61, the sprawled, bloody body of the dead man lying on the front seat of his car, and a crowd gathering to gape; the complete lack of cooperation between the city police and the county sheriff's department in their war against drugs-related crime. Each department refused to deputize the other's officers so that a suspect being pursued, say, out of the town into the county by the city police could escape just by crossing the county boundary.

Guns, of course, are readily available and just as readily used. Nighttime gunshots are common in Clarksdale. Sometimes they signify a dead armadillo, shot-gunned while it dug up the flowers in a local garden; more often it is a dead drug dealer, gunned down while he sat in his Buick. We met a Clarksdale police officer, walking a poodle around the neat verges of suburban Clarksdale. She claimed to us to have been the first white female to become an officer in the Clarksdale police, but her first few days at work had already shown how hard acceptance was going to be amongst the other officers. The Clarksdale police have none of the glamorous hardware that you see on television cop shows – she had not been issued with the latest plastic Glock automatic but with an ancient .38 revolver with a faulty hammer. They did not even have a enough bullets to give her a full complement.

■

Skip Henderson was sitting in a big armchair, feet up on the porch rail, when we met him, lording over his little bit of Clarksdale like a Yankee conqueror come down to tell these careless Southerners how to make some money out of their blues heritage. Which is exactly what he had come to do, although it would be unfair not to recognize that he had honourable intentions and was a genuine fan of blues and Delta culture.

It wasn't even his porch. It belonged to Panny Mayfield, a local journalist and photographer. When we paid a visit, she was still in her office organizing the town's third Tennessee Williams Festival, which this year was to coincide with the launching of a commemorative stamp. For Panny and Clarksdale it was quite a coup that they had managed to persuade the US Postal Service to launch the stamp in Clarksdale rather than New Orleans, which had a much higher Tennessee Williams profile and was a major tourist city, with the resources to finance a major celebration like this one.

Skip used to run a music store in New Jersey and was a guitar dealer of some repute. He is also a blues fan and set up the Mount Zion Memorial Fund which raised money and organized the erection of memorial stones at the neglected grave sites of several Delta bluesmen. He had already donated his large collection of guitars to the Delta Blues Museum. His dedication was rewarded in 1992 when he received the Early Wright Award for the preservation, promotion, and perpetuation of blues at that year's Sunflower River Blues Festival. By 1995 he was looking to settle permanently in Clarksdale and had big plans for the old railway station, which he had bought.

The station is a striking, old building and an important one in the history of the movement of blues from the Delta up to the Northern cities. It was from here that thousands of unemployed plantation and farm workers left for the North, heading for the industrial cities of Detroit, St Louis and especially Chicago. The exodus has been called the biggest unforced migration in the world. Between 1910 and 1970, 6.5 million people left the South and headed for the industrial cities of the North, 5 million of these between 1940 and 1970. In 1940, over three-quarters of the country's black population still lived in the South but that was to change over the following 30 years as the introduction of new mechanized farming methods made the plantations far less labour-intensive.

The sharecropping system died and left the unneeded sharecroppers to fend for themselves – there was almost no other work in the Delta so usually this meant heading up North. The row tractor was first introduced by International Harvester in 1922 but its impact was small. What was really needed in order for the plantation owners to become less reliant on their labour was a mass-produced mechanized picker. Richard Hopson, whose plantation was just outside Clarksdale, was one of the most active movers in the mechanization process: 'I strongly advocate the farmers of the Delta . . . changing to complete mechanized farming,' he wrote in 1944 and, interestingly, he went on to stress not only the economic benefits of mechanization but also the benefits in alleviating 'our racial problem'.

In 1944 he demonstrated a prototype International Harvester picker at his plantation. He showed that it could do the work of 50 manual pickers and that each bale of cotton cost him $5.26 to pick as opposed to $39.41 for a hand-picked bale. The economic argument was overwhelming and 300 of his pickers were put out of work immediately. By 1947 International Harvester were mass-producing the self-propelled one-row picker. Ironically their Chicago factory where the machines were made was largely staffed by cheap immigrant labour . . . from the Delta. In 1950 only 7 per cent of the Delta's cotton had not been hand-picked; by the end of the decade the figure was over half and by 1967, 95 per cent of Delta cotton was machine-picked. During the same period the Delta's rural farm population fell by 54 per cent. In the 1950s the widespread introduction of chemical weedkillers eliminated the need for weed-pulling, which had been the last refuge for Delta farm-labourers struggling to find work (Nicholas Lemann, *The Promised Land*).

Muddy Waters was one of those 6.5 million migrants. In May 1943 he asked for a pay rise from 22½ cents an hour to 25 cents (Robert Palmer, *Deep Blues*). His request was refused and, knowing that his sister and her husband were already in Chicago, he caught a four o'clock train from the railroad station that Friday and was in Chicago by Saturday morning. He wore his best suit and didn't take much else with him: a small suitcase, his acoustic guitar, and the rhythmic, swinging versions of Robert Johnson's Delta blues that he played. These blues were soon to take on the electric hardness of the city and be transformed into the music that captured the imagination of a succession of rock and pop musicians all over the world.

So the station at Clarksdale does have an important place in blues history. But that is history – the past. Skip Henderson aims to give it a role in the present. He bought the station on the spur of the moment and put the $3,600 down payment on his credit card! He raised the rest of the money within six weeks and had soon negotiated a deal with the city of Clarksdale whereby they owned the building and he leased it back from them. He also made sure that he had $150,000 to spend on a state-of-the-art sound system!

He calls the project Bluesland and plans to make it an eating, shopping, and entertainment complex. Blueprints have been drawn up which retain the extensive marble and wood fittings that make the station such a beautiful old building but transform it into a music club where the best international blues and country stars will be able to play, and where local musicians can have a comfortable, regular venue to show off their talents. The complex will also have a bar and a restaurant, and shop units for local entrepreneurs to lease. Skip's dream is to serve top-quality food and drink, to bring a touch of cosmopolitan epicureanism to the town: 'You'll be able to get cappuccino in Clarksdale!'

Music will have to be the basis upon which any revitalization of Clarksdale and the surrounding counties is built. Not only does it provide the cultural history on which the likes of the Blues Museum are based but it is also the main contemporary attraction for tourists drawn to the area. The Wesley Jefferson Band and the Stone Gas Band are two of Clarksdale's premier bands. Arthneice 'Gasman' Jones leads the Stone Gas Band and he is a real eccentric with a love of what he calls 'Delta dance blues' and ideas about blues timing and chord changes that are truly from another world. Unfortunately we were never able to meet up with Arthneice – we were always on the same planet at different times or, more often, Arthneice was on a different planet altogether. His band includes former protégés of Johnnie Billington and Howard Stovall, the

Yale-educated plantation-owner's son who had given Billy Gibbons investment advice.

Wesley 'Junebug' Jefferson leads his band with the relaxed authority of a benevolent father and he needs to because the Wesley Jefferson Band contains such a frothy mix of musical personalities, such a wealth of wilful musical talent. They have their own album out now and Wesley himself deserves much of the credit for creating and holding together the band for long enough to make the album. Leading lights in the local blues scene, like Lorenzo Nicholson and C.V. Veal, have passed through the band and on special occasions will sometimes return. Their regular haunt is the Do Drop Inn in Shelby, a few miles to the south of Clarksdale. It is a long, low building, about 7ft high with bare wooden beams supporting the roof. The signs on its walls are hand-painted and feature pictures of Playboy bunnies and exhortations to 'Party!', 'Dynamite!' and 'Dance!' The lighting is minimal – a single bulb above the stage, a police-car-style flashing light in one corner, and the neon from the Miller and Old Bud beer signs.

The place was packed when I saw them play there. The tables and chairs on either side of the narrow corridor of space leading to the stage were all occupied and the bar was doing a busy trade in their very cheap bottled Budweiser. Unfortunately there is no real dance area, just the narrow strip between the tables and an equally narrow strip at the front by the stage. When the band cranked it up about four songs into their first set, couples crowded their vigorous dancing into this constricted space.

Everybody was there: Skip Henderson lurked at the back of the room, beer in hand and baseball cap pushed far back on his head; John Ruskey's eager assistants and their friends had occupied a table in a prime spot down near the front; and Panny Mayfield abandoned a Tennessee Williams Festival cocktail party to catch the band's last set. She made quite an entrance, having been stopped by a policeman at the junction just outside the club. It was a Sunday night and it was John Ruskey's birthday so we all had a reason to celebrate.

There are enough aspiring leaders in the band to start a whole stable of Clarksdale blues groups. Charity singles have been recorded with fewer guitar stars than there are in this band. The leading lights on the night we saw the band were James 'Super Chikan' Johnson and Michael 'Dr Mike' James. 'Super Chikan' is Big Jack Johnson's nephew and shares some of Jack's virtuosity and flights of imagination, even if, as yet, he lacks some of his uncle's subtlety of touch. Dr Mike expressed a wider range of emotions through his playing and has a quieter voice but a more moving one. John Ruskey played keyboards and accepted the 'Happy birthdays' and cheering with the same quizzical smile and good grace that are his usual demeanour. The 'Mississippi Junebug' himself sang on several of the numbers but, by and large, stayed in the background and watched his guitar stars as a father watches his talented but wild family.

'Super Chikan' played his big, garish heavy-metal guitar with a cheerful swagger and managed to keep his pipe alight throughout. He completed a strutting version of *Itchin'* by inviting a succession of girls up from the audience to scratch his back! The repertoire was blues standards including Freddie King's *The Shuffle*, *Stormy Monday*, and *Mustang Sally.*

The band's music was a hip-shaking mixture of classic songs and self-penned numbers that update traditional Delta musical motifs with thoroughly up-to-date lyrics. It is made for juke-joints like the Do Drop Inn: it is perfectly complemented by beer, dancing, and uninhibited hedonism and should prove a heady attraction for the tourists that come to Bluesland and the Museum.

Skip Henderson has gone North, heading back to New Jersey. Perhaps the promise of good coffee was not enough to outweigh the familiar attractions of his Northern home. The Bluesland project has been taken over by Bill Barth, the blues aficionado who managed Skip James in the 1960s. The club was due to open in 1997.

Muddy's famous shack, the same one that the Muddywood guitar was made from, has been moved. The Blues Museum wanted to set it up in front of their building. Instead it has been taken on a promotional tour of the US (it even made an appearance at the Atlanta Olympics) by the Disney Corporation and Isaac Tigrett's House of Blues organization. As Bill Barth says, though, 'They can put it on the White House lawn, but Isaac better remember that a house is not a home!' (interview *Paul Jones R 'n' B Show*, BBC Radio).

A sceptic might see Clarksdale and its blues history as a kind of microcosm of blues in general – a music with a rich past and strong back catalogue, strictly retrospective yet creating a current scene. A traditional museum, a repository of the past, would usually reinforce this view. But the reality is more complicated. In Clarksdale the movers and shakers of the community respect the past, the weight of blues history that surrounds them, but the future that they are trying to build is more than just a theme park for blues: the Delta Blues Education Fund is showing kids that it is not only rap that can articulate their frustrations, and the younger musicians of Clarksdale are playing music that updates and revives the blues form. Moreover, everyone we met in Clarksdale was trying to break down the long-established walls that divided their society on racial lines, to combine the diverse strands that make up the Delta's history rather than emphasizing the divisions of the past. The museum itself is closely involved in creating and encouraging new music and musicians as well as cataloguing and recording the lives and work of past musicians.

Epilogue

T HE BLUES MUSIC that I found in the Delta and in Memphis (and I consider that it's high time the city became an honorary part of Mississippi) marked the culmination of a 15-year search. It was a search for the purest and most nakedly emotional music, the ultimate blues – the 'bluest' blues, if you like – and it felt just as difficult to find, just as elusive, as treasure at the end of a rainbow. The treasure was 'real' blues: authentic music, not adulterated by the commercial appeal of a 'crossover' audience and not diluted by the alien experiences of white suburbanites from Surrey or from the University of Chicago.

Of course, the reality was more confusing: there were no clear-cut 'originators' and 'imitators', just musicians adopting and adapting the music of their predecessors, as they had always done. White appropriation and profit from black artistry was not a cultural theft that was specific to blues but a manifestation of a wider system of racial relationships that infected all of US society.

The contemporary music of the Delta is certainly some of the 'bluest' blues: it is as deeply felt and as passionately delivered as any. But it has survived – retaining its old audiences and finding new ones – with help from all kinds of places, some of them a long way (metaphorically and literally) from the Delta. In Clarksdale, for example, the parts of the blues continuum that are contributing to the town's potential for revival – the bands themselves, the Blues Museum, and the Delta Blues Education Fund – all draw, in part at least, on sources other than traditional, indigenous blues culture. The promise and potential of Clarksdale exist because different parts of its community are pulling together to create a new future – the same ones that, in the past, so divided the community and, in the process, gave rise to the blues.

■

'It's not dying here!'

Most blues writing reveres the musicians of the past and emphasizes the creativity and ability of the stars of the pre-war era and of the blues 'revival' in the late 1950s and 60s. This reverence for dead or dying stars insinuates that these artists, strumming anciently on their back porches, are the last practitioners of a dying art, and that the musical tradition they have inherited from their predecessors will be buried with them. The implication is that the music is moribund and that the voyage of the blues – starting with its musical antecedents in Africa – from the Delta to Chicago, and from there to the rest of the world, will soon end. In the treasure chest at the end of my blues rainbow was the discovery that this insinuation was mistaken. The blues scene of the Delta was not moribund: for every old musician who played the music and talked the language of the old days there were two or three younger ones who burned with the vigour of their musical passions and bore witness to a scene that was *contemporary*, alive, and defiantly of the Delta. And there are many more Mississippi musicians who we did not manage to interview or hear playing – Cedell Davis, Eugene Powell, Eddie Cusic, Hezekiah Early, Arthneice 'Gasman' Jones, and Lonnie Shields, to name just a few.

The scene is still resolutely 'local': the blues is keenly appreciated by the same local audiences whose fathers, mothers, grandparents, and cousins danced and cavorted the weekend away when Charley Patton, Robert Johnson, and Elmore James were playing in the Delta. The music they listen to still performs a role that is much more than just a means of entertainment. Bluesmen are still social commentators: the instinctive, outspoken voices of reaction for a whole subclass of US society that does not have access to more considered or more formal means of communication.

I learned more about the diversities and divisions of contemporary US society and about the legacies of its history during my trips to Mississippi than I have from hundreds of films, TV shows, and novels (let alone history books). The Delta's blues musicians still have stories to tell that speak as eloquently of their situation as the soul musicians of the 1960s did in the era of civil rights activity and as the rap artists of urban America still do. The concerns of contemporary Delta blues artists are still impregnated (albeit often not consciously) with the inarticulate anger and resentment of nearly three centuries of slavery or economic enslavement.

The vitality of Mississippi blues today is an invigorating antidote to the seeming sameness of some contemporary blues that often seems to have been recorded on a production line where the rocked-out, guitar-heavy sound of pseudo-Chicago blues is the only permitted end-product. Contemporary Mississippi blues reinstates the pre-eminence of the individual voice of each artist – their songs and musicianship convey their own specific blues, not that of a generic factory product. Thus the guitar antics of Jack Johnson or Booba Barnes have a story to relate and an emotion to communicate as well as music to dance to.

Musical Esperanto

The language of the blues started out as the means of response, or reaction, for the poor, black sharecroppers who had long been the most straitened subclass in the poorest state of the world's richest country. Their experiences were exacerbated versions of similar, universal human troubles. Thus the language that they developed was ripe for understanding, assimilation, and adoption by a wider, international audience. In doing so it picked up fresh nuances and new colloquialisms to become a new language, a kind of musical esperanto for the whole world. It still articulates the troubles of its listeners and its creators – universal human concerns of dissatisfaction, alienation, and lost love.

Down in Mississippi

Back in the Delta the economic and social conditions that engendered blues still exist, but in some towns there are signs of improvement. Clarksdale, for example, is showing a new way forward in which local blues is playing a vital regenerative part in the everyday life of the town. It is sustaining life and entertaining the people (as it always did) – providing a strong dose of medicine for the accumulated ills and sufferings.

If this Mississippi medicine is not too strong for outside tastes, the latest flowering of Delta blues may find another, new, world-wide audience and become a palliative far beyond its birthplace. Clarksdale doesn't mind – it doesn't need an international audience as long as its blues continues to bring the community together and alleviates some of its ills. For, in Mississippi today, the blues is doing what it has always done.

DISCOGRAPHY

T HIS LIST COVERS the musicians featured in the text (more specifically, those who have had recordings released) and the others most frequently referred to. It is based on *my own* collection and it is not intended that the list should be regarded as comprehensive. Some of the records listed are out of print; equally some have been reissued several times on different labels and in different parts of the world.

For more comprehensive blues discographies try Mike Leadbitter and Neil Slaven's *Blues Records 1943–1970*, Paul Oliver's *The Blackwell Guide to Blues Records* or Miller Freeman's *All Music Guide to the Blues*. More up to date, and also hugely enjoyable in his inimitably opinionated way, is Charles Shaar Murray's *Blues on CD: The Essential Guide.*

Roosevelt 'Booba' Barnes & the Playboys: 'The Heartbroken Man', Rooster Blues

The Blues Brothers: 'Original Soundtrack Recording', Atlantic

Booker T. and the MGs: 'Green Onions', Atlantic

R.L. Burnside: 'Bad Luck City', Fat Possum; 'Too Bad Jim', Fat Possum; 'Mr Wizard', Fat Possum

Scott Dunbar: 'From Lake Mary', Ahura Mazda

The Fieldstones: 'Memphis Blues Today', Highwater

Willie Foster: 'I Found Joy', Palindrome
There is another album featuring Willie Foster – the recordings he made with the Midge Marsden band. But you may have to go to New Zealand to find it!

Frank Frost: 'Jelly Roll King', Charly

Al Green: 'Greatest Hits,' Hi

Buddy Guy: 'Hold That Plane!', Vanguard; 'Slippin' In', Silvertone; 'Damn Right I Got The Blues', Silvertone; 'Feels Like Rain', Silvertone
There are also several collections of Buddy Guy's 1960s material.

Jessie Mae Hemphill: 'Feelin' Good', Highwater
There are also a couple of hard-to-come-by French albums by Jessie Mae.

The Hollywood All Stars: 'Hard Hitting Blues From Memphis', Highwater

John Lee Hooker: 'The Best of John Lee Hooker', Music Club; 'The Healer', Silvertone; 'Mr Lucky', Silvertone; 'Boom, Boom', Point Blank

Lightnin' Hopkins: 'How Many More Years I Got', Ace

Howlin' Wolf: 'His Greatest Sides', Volume 1, Chess; 'The London Howlin' Wolf Sessions', Chess

Elmore James: 'The Original Meteor and Flair Sides', Ace; 'One Way Out', Charly

The Wesley Jefferson Band: 'Delta Blues, Live From The Do Drop Inn', Repap

The Jelly Roll Kings: 'Rockin' The Juke Joint Down', Earwig

Big Jack Johnson: 'The Oil Man', Earwig; 'Daddy, When is Mama Coming Home?', Earwig; 'We Got to Stop This Killin'', MC Records

Robert Johnson: 'King of the Delta Blues Singers', Vols. 1 & 2, Blue Diamond

Junior Kimborough & the Soul Blues Boys: 'All Night Long', Fat Possum; 'Sad Days, Lonely Nights', Fat Possum

Albert King: 'I'll Play the Blues for You', Stax; 'Lovejoy', Stax; 'King of the Blues Guitar', Atlantic

B.B. King: 'Blues Summit', MCA; 'Best of B.B. King', MCA; 'Live at the Regal', MCA
For the full B.B. King experience get the 4-CD collection which covers his career from the first single in 1949: 'King of the Blues', MCA

Freddie King: 'Taking Care of Business', Charly

Little Jimmy King: 'Little Jimmy King and the Memphis Soul Survivors', Bullseye Blues; 'Something Inside of Me', Bullseye Blues

Little Walter: 'The Best of Little Walter', Chess

Magic Sam: 'Easy Baby', Charly

David Malone & the Sugar Bears: 'I Got the Dog in Me', Fat Possum

Jack Owens: 'It Must Have Been the Devil', Testament

Lonnie Pitchford: 'All Around Man', Rooster Blues

Otis Redding: 'Otis Blue', Stax; 'History of Otis Redding', Atco

The Rolling Stones: 'Rolled Gold, The Very Best of the Rolling Stones',
    Decca

Otis Rush: 'Otis Rush 1956–1958', Paula

James 'Son' Thomas: 'Gateway to the Delta', Rustron

George Thorogood and the Destroyers: 'Move It on Over', Sonet

Various: 'Clarksdale, Mississippi, Coahoma The Blues', Rooster Blues;
    'Deep Blues', Atlantic; 'The Story of the Blues', Columbia; 'Yazoo
    Delta . . . Blues and Spirituals', Prestige

T-Bone Walker: 'T-Bone Jumps Again', Charly

Muddy Waters: 'They Call Me Muddy Waters', Instant; 'Down on Stovall's
    Plantation', Testament; 'The London Muddy Waters Sessions', Chess;
    'Hard Again', Blue Sky
    Muddy has also had the CD box-set treatment: 'The Chess Box',
    MCA/Chess

Sonny Boy Williamson: 'Chess Masters: Sonny Boy Williamson', Chess

O. V. Wright. 'Gone For Good', Charly

ZZ Top: 'Best of ZZ Top', Warner Brothers

Mail order is the best option for those hard-to-come-by rarities. Try:

Red Lick Records
Porthmadog
Gwynedd
LL49 9DJ
UK
(01766 512151)

*B*IBLIOGRAPHY

T HE FOLLOWING TITLES are only a selection of those written on the blues – but do represent the principal titles on my bookshelf. Publishers listed are those of the editions I consulted and read; so there is often a parallel US or UK publisher, respectively, to the one listed here.

Bane, Michael, *White Boy Singin' The Blues*, Da Capo, New York, 1982

Booth, Stanley, *Rythm Oil*, Jonathan Cape, London, 1991

Charters, Samuel, *The Legacy Of The Blues*, Da Capo, New York, 1977

Cobb, James, *The Most Southern Place On Earth*, Oxford University Press, New York, 1992

Davis, Francis, *History of the Blues*, Secker & Warburg, London, 1995

Ferris, William, *Blues From The Delta*, Da Capo, New York, 1978

Guralnick, Peter, *Feel Like Going Home*, Harper & Row, New York, 1971

Kell, Charles, *Urban Blues*, University of Chicago Press, Chicago, 1991

Larkin, Colin (ed.), *The Guinness Who's Who of Blues*, Guinness, Enfield, 1993

Leadbitter, Mike & Slaven, Neil (eds.), *Blues Records 1943–1970*, London, 1970

Lemann, Nicholas, *The Promised Land*, Macmillan, London, 1991

Lomax, Alan, *The Land Where The Blues Began*, Minerva, London, 1994

Miller Freeman's *All Music Guide to the Blues*, Miller Freeman, San Francisco, 1996

The Wesley Jefferson Band at the Do Drop Inn.
Panny Mayfield

Murray, Charles Shaar, *Blues on CD: The Essential Guide*, Kyle Cathie, London, 1993

Oliver, Paul, *Blues Fell This Morning*, Cambridge University Press, Cambridge, 1990
— *The Story Of The Blues*, Cresset Press, London, 1969
— (ed.) *The Blackwell Guide to Blues Music*, Blackwell, Oxford, 1989

Palmer, Robert, *Deep Blues*, Penguin, London, 1982

Sawyer, Charles, *B.B. King: The Authorized Biography*, Blandford, Poole, 1981

Welding, Pete & Byron, Toby (eds.), *Bluesland*, Dutton, London, 1991

Magazines

Invaluable information has been gained from numerous articles, reviews, interviews, and obituaries in various issues of *Living Blues* magazine in the USA. Other useful magazines include *Juke Blues*, *Folk Roots*, *Blues & Rhythm: The Gospel Truth*, and *Blueprint* in the UK and such magazines as *Blues News* in Germany.

*I*ndex